First published by Stonebridge Books, an imprint of
Jacana Media (Pty) Ltd in 2011

10 Orange Street
Sunnyside
Auckland Park 2092
South Africa
+2711 628 3200
www.jacana.co.za

© Tyrrel Fairhead, 2011

All rights reserved.

ISBN 978-1-4314-0248-9
Job No. 001563

Cover design publicide
Photos © Eric Miller emiller@iafrica.com
Set in Sabon 11/15pt
Printed by Ultra Litho (Pty) Ltd Johannesburg

See a complete list of Jacana titles at www.jacana.co.za

The MADIBA MINDSET

Your Own FREEDOM CHARTER

Tyrrel FAIRHEAD

Author's motivation

INITIALLY MOTIVATED BY A concern that the teachings, wisdom and insights of Nelson Mandela may go to waste and be lost to future generations, Tyrrel Fairhead was moved to acknowledge and record it all. He studied the material, unpacked it, and has presented it in a form that can be used and modelled by all. He decided to name this programme MadibaMindset, as a way of honouring the teachings of Nelson Mandela and his fellow political prisoners. This programme is therefore an interpretation of how the Mindset was practised, and the understanding of how to make it applicable to 'normal' living conditions.

Contents

Preface vii

The goal of this book xi

Reading suggestions xii

Introduction xv

Chapter 1: Why do it? 1

Chapter 2: The core of the MadibaMindset 19

Chapter 3: Conviction creates energy 37

Chapter 4: Write your own freedom charter 55

Chapter 5: What you can do 67

Chapter 6: How you can do it 79

Chapter 7: Is it final or can we aim for Chapter 11? 101

Appendix A: Aiming higher 112

Appendix B: Important readers' questions
and author's replies 118

Acknowledgements 119

Suggested reading 121

Preface

MIKE NICOL
(co-author of *Mandela – The Authorised Portrait*)

THE IDEA OF NELSON MANDELA has begun to take on a significance possibly greater than the man himself. There are few individuals of whom this can be said in their lifetimes, but for Mandela it is true. He has come to embody concepts of tolerance and forgiveness that in their depth and magnanimity have even astonished those who know him well.

But, as if these ideals – founded on the premises of African ubuntu (that our humanity is confirmed by other people) and universal compassion – are not enough, Mandela also stands for the democratic and human rights tenets upon which South African society is constitutionally founded. In addition he has considerable respect for the rule of law.

Ironically, of course, Mandela has also held the opposite of these positions at certain times in his life. He was one of the leading forces behind the formation of Umkhonto we Sizwe, the armed wing of the African National Congress, and therefore a proponent of violence. There are other instances, for example during his negotiations with the South African government in the mid-1980s, when he was inclined to act autocratically and even, once, incurred the censure of his comrades. Similar moments occurred during cabinet sessions once the ANC was in power. And, most famously, although as a lawyer he has championed due process, he regularly broke laws he regarded as unjust and inhumane. Perhaps one of the most important elements of Mandela's legacy is his ability to hold two opposing ideas without apparent contradiction.

Mandela's life is about complexity. About seeing the myriad causes that might inform an event, and this has led to his generous world view. Had he been a man who viewed matters in black and white, he would have emerged from Robben Island embittered and angry. In truth he did emerge angry, angry at the futility and waste of the apartheid years, but he did not let this anger obstruct his desire to build a new nation. Instead the anger was sublimated because he realised it would have meant a prison of another kind. To escape this darker self-inflicted prison, the anger and the waste were put aside even if they were not forgotten. Freedom lay in understanding and forgiveness. It also lay, as he well knew, in education or an openness to acquiring knowledge.

Throughout his life education has been a major concern to Mandela. Often his own education came at a price. There were times when he went hungry in pursuance of his legal studies; there were times when his teachers even tried to dissuade and fail him. For Mandela, education was a way to a better life, a fulfilled life. The MadibaMindset is about education, about acquiring knowledge and self-knowledge. 'Education is the great engine of personal development,' Mandela told the author Reginald McKnight. 'It is what we make out of what we have, not what we are given, that separates one person from another.' This book describes an empowering method to exemplify that dictum.

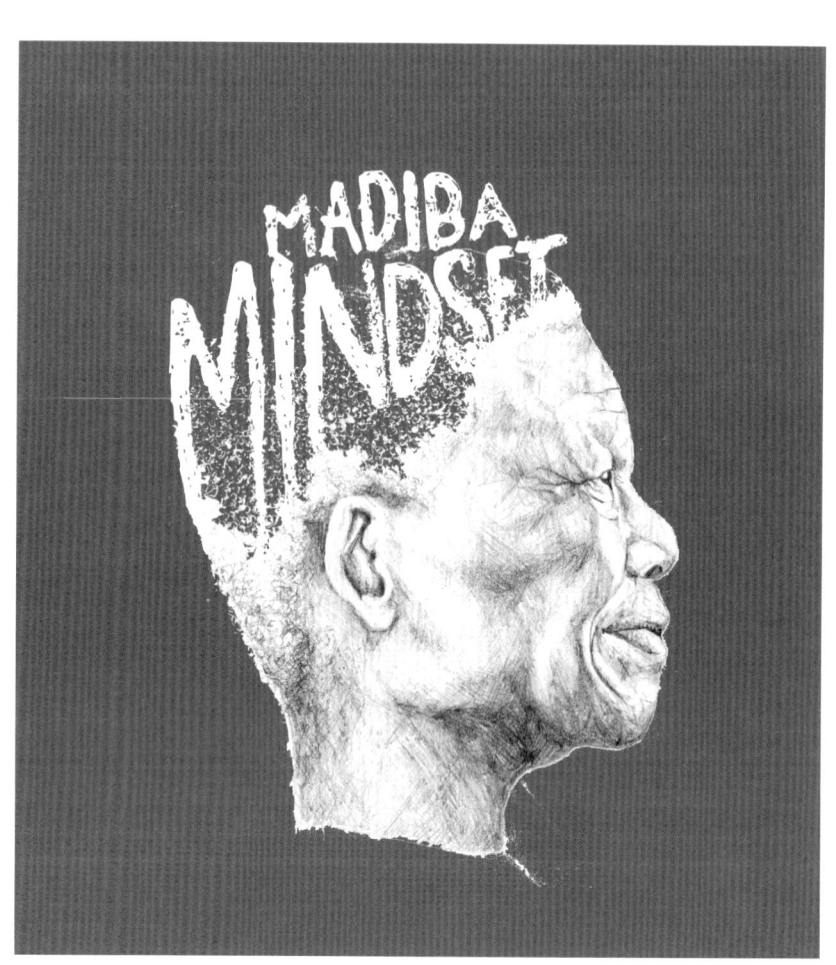

The goal of this book

The only adequate way in which we can truly express our gratitude for his lifetime's contribution is for every one of us to work every day to seek to follow his example.
KOFI ANNAN
Foreword: *Mandela – The Authorised Portrait*

MY GOAL IS TO PROVIDE a practical tool for all to respectfully follow the example of Nelson Mandela. I also wish to acknowledge all those who contributed to this great historic precedent. As Richard Stengel points out in *Mandela's Way*, it goes far back and includes many people not referred to here, people as diverse as Winston Churchill, Walter Sisulu, Oliver Tambo, Julius Nyerere, Haile Selassie, and an English headmaster. Mandela himself has always been the first to share credit and acknowledge the influence of others in the development of his thinking. He is proud to admit that he stands on the shoulders of others who have gone before.

To encourage and enable readers to follow his example is the only goal of this book.

Political beliefs, and claims to ownership, have been expressed about segments of the history of the World Heritage Site that is Robben Island and our role models who were imprisoned there. In the context of governments and current events, this book too can be politicised. I do, however, respect the many different beliefs that form part of other people's models of the world and commend any model or belief that helps us to follow Mandela's example. It is also worth noting that Mandela is remarkably open to new and good ideas. He is not in the least sectarian. On Robben Island, political prisoners did not just come from Mandela's own political party. There were even prisoners from Namibia. Mandela's great talent was to make them see what it was that they had in common – and to try to find the very best in each person.

On the following pages I have identified some of the vital lessons that Mandela and his fellows learned from their convictions and their own role models. We can benefit from this and can gain immeasurably by following these examples. Use this book as a recipe and many small efforts and resources can synergistically lead to greater results!

Reading suggestions

- Reference works are italicised. For publication details of these volumes, see the Suggested reading.
- Some 'Quotation' marks are not direct quotes but rather signify words that suggest much more than their literal meaning- look out for these. For instance the word 'convicted' implies a level of conviction so great that one is absolutely willing to do everything necessary to achieve it.
- **Bold** denotes an issue or statement worthy of the reader's special attention.
- 'Dream' headings may mean much more after you read Chapter 4. Until then, simply think imaginatively about what follows these headings.
- All text contained in stand-alone sheets at the ends of chapters highlights exercises you can do to maximise your benefits from this book. Readers may become too engrossed to stop and do the exercises. By all means return to do them when you finish reading.
- The pictures at the beginnings of chapters are presented out of their original context and presented to stimulate constructive thought, together with the quotations below the chapter headings.

Introduction

[South Africa has a] great deal to be proud of in its struggle for freedom ... the problems that remain are no less daunting than those already overcome.
FRANCIS WILSON
Dinosaurs, Diamonds and Democracy (p. 120)

UNTIL EARLY 1990 many people believed that South Africa was on the road to civil war, war that would finally unleash black anger against white racism. Four years later, Nelson Mandela was sworn in as the country's first black president. Much happened during those four years, beginning with Nelson Mandela's release from prison after 27 years and ending with the country's first-ever free and fair multiracial elections.

Many people see this relatively peaceful transition from oppressive apartheid to a modern democracy, without a civil war, as nothing less than a miracle. No doubt it is. Nevertheless, it is a miracle based on decades of preparation and firmly held convictions by many people who suffered under one of the world's more 'successful' oppressive regimes. An essential part of this miracle is how many of the leaders of these oppressed people used their long incarcerations in prison, mostly on Robben Island, to continue preparing for the time when they would be called upon to lead their country – even as their convictions were tested day after painful day.

Although Robben Island was not a death camp, conditions

were extremely oppressive and designed to destroy the morale and dedication of the inmates. These political prisoners had all been given long sentences, many life sentences, following their conviction for political offences. The island is in the icy Atlantic Ocean that surrounds Cape Town, and the magnificent Table Mountain is clearly visible from it. Cape Town is beautiful and life there is good. The seductive freedom of life in the city is visible to all on Robben Island, but it could not be reached by the prisoners because the ocean is bitterly cold and sharks swim in its strong currents. The cells were cramped, punishingly cold in winter and severely hot in summer. The guards' job was to treat prisoners harshly. Inmates toiled by day in the stone and lime quarries, often in the glare of the sun or in cold rainy conditions accompanied by strong winds. Rations were meagre and unpleasant. Despite these conditions the political prisoners on Robben Island continued to believe that they were the new South African democratic government-in-waiting. They regarded their stay as an opportunity to prepare for this job. Nobel laureate and Archbishop Emeritus Desmond Tutu explained, in *Mandela – The Authorised Portrait*, that 'Suffering can of course embitter the one who suffers. But in many instances it can ennoble the sufferer.' (p. 9)

The programme presented in this book is based on how many South African heroes achieved what they did. Initially motivated by a concern that these strategies may go to waste and be lost to future generations, I was moved to acknowledge the material, to unpack it, and to present it in a form that can be used and modelled by all. I decided to name this programme MadibaMindset, as a way of honouring the teachings of Nelson Mandela and his fellow political prisoners.

I make no claim to ownership of the ideas, nor to having invented the material as practised on Robben Island. However, I believe that the way I have analysed and presented the available public and archived information about the political prisoners, and combined it with the recorded experiences of other international examples, timeless universal teachings, current psychological research and practical business ideas, is new, if not unique.

Introduction

The programme as presented is both similar and different to how Nelson Mandela and his colleagues practised it while incarcerated. The main reason for this is that I have never spent time locked up in an apartheid prison like Robben Island. This programme is therefore my own interpretation of how the Mindset was practised, and my understanding of how to make it applicable to 'normal' living conditions.

I am convinced that the strategies used in South Africa's negotiated revolution comprise valuable and relatively unused resources available to governments, non-governmental organisations, businesses and individuals. This programme has, therefore, been developed to make these strategies available to you, the reader, who can **use them productively**. The MadibaMindset is a way of escaping from the mental prison that inhibits you, preventing you from being able to rise above present circumstances and challenges. The pleasing result is that individuals and organisations can uncover, articulate and demonstrate the beliefs, values, habits, strategies and structures that empower them to live and work in accord with their convictions every day.

The term 'Madiba' is a clan name of the Xhosa people in South Africa. According to babynology.com the first person to whom this name was given was a Thembu chief who ruled the Transkei (where Mandela was born and the original land of the Xhosa) in the eighteenth century. Many of Nelson Mandela's philosophies and principles appear to stem from the culture, beliefs and values of the Madiba clan and related Xhosa groups. Two fundamental beliefs critical to the peaceful transition of power in South Africa were formed during his childhood observations at the Great Place of Chief Jongintaba Dalindyebo, then the regent of the Thembu people. These are his belief in democracy and his belief in an inclusive leadership style. In his autobiography, *Long Walk to Freedom*, Mandela explains that his 'later notions of leadership were profoundly influenced by observing the regent and his court. I watched and learned from the tribal meetings that were regularly held at the Great Place.' (p. 18)

To this day some people still question why Mandela, apparently such a convicted leader, did not always speak out as strongly on certain issues as they would have liked him to have done. They also question why he seldom defended himself when he was attacked by those who disagreed with him in public. An answer can once again be found in what he learned from the regent: '... and [the regent would explain] why he had summoned them. From that point on, he would not utter another word until the meeting was nearing its end. Everyone who wanted to speak did so. It was democracy in its purest form. At first, I was astonished by the vehemence – and candour – with which some people criticised the regent. He was not above criticism – in fact, he was often the principle target of it. But no matter how flagrant the charge, the regent simply listened, not defending himself, showing no emotion at all.' (pp. 18–19)

And his democratic leadership style he explains as follows: 'As a leader, I have always followed the principles I first saw demonstrated by the regent at the Great Place. I have always endeavoured to listen to what each and every person in a discussion had to say before venturing my own opinion. Oftentimes my own opinion will simply represent a consensus of what I heard in the discussion. I always remember the regent's axiom: a leader, he said, is like a shepherd. He stays behind the flock, letting the most nimble go out ahead, whereupon the others follow, not realising that all along they are being directed from behind.' (p. 19)

Also notice how what he observed as a child about democracy and leadership in action combined to create his determination to fight for democracy, and not merely majority rule, as many other resistance leaders demanded: 'Democracy meant all men were to be heard, and a decision was taken together as a people. Majority rule was a foreign notion. A minority was not to be crushed by a majority.' (p. 19)

As Mandela came to embody these principles, people began calling him Madiba as a term of respect and affection. Although the term Madiba is historically bigger than Nelson Mandela, it has come to symbolise the man and his beliefs, principles and convictions, and ultimately, his actions. Nelson Mandela is but

Introduction

one of many who strived to overthrow the apartheid regime. Nevertheless, he has come to represent the miracle of the relatively peaceful transition. He has been described by some as a secular saint and recognised by others, especially erstwhile foes, as a master tactician.

This combination of secular saint, master tactician and all the other admirable habits convinced me that it would be appropriate to name this programme MadibaMindset. It is furthermore my way of honouring the man and his compatriots, and the dream-turned-reality that they embodied. It also serves as a reminder to all that 'miracles' are indeed possible when we **live with conviction**. Not all of us can live as convicted as Nelson Mandela. To understand what true conviction is we can benefit by considering the words he spoke at his treason trial, held in 1963 and 1964, after which he was sentenced to life in prison:

'During my lifetime I have dedicated myself to this struggle of the African people. I have fought against white domination, and I have fought against black domination. I have cherished the ideal of a democratic and free society in which all persons live together in harmony and with equal opportunities. It is an ideal which I hope to live for and to achieve. But if needs be, it is an ideal for which I am prepared to die.' This statement was made from the dock in the Rivonia Trial at the Pretoria Supreme Court on 20 April 1964. At the time the death penalty was often applied in these cases.

Why is this programme relevant today?

As you read further you will discover answers to this question in the context of your own lives. On a more general level, I stress the following issues:

The perilous state of the world economy and the health of the planet have highlighted just how wasteful current government, business and organisational practices have become in the use of capital, human energy and natural resources. As the new normal economy develops into the future we will all need and learn to **do more with less**. It is therefore essential that we now discard the inappropriate practices of the past and embrace the future with new ways of thinking, strategising and doing.

What transpired on Robben Island during the last decades of the twentieth century is the best example from recent history, and probably world history, of how to turn a destructive system into a productive experience. The Robben Island experience shows clearly that it is possible to create a better future even as we find ourselves in a system specifically designed to stimulate a waste of emotional energy and restrict access to money and other 'necessary' tangible resources.

You can live a more successful life, however you define it, by applying the MadibaMindset. This can lead to improvement in the way individuals, organisations, communities and even nations operate.

There are also unanswered questions like: how much more can South Africa achieve if it embraces and popularises the MadibaMindset philosophies and principles? How much can the South African education system and people achieve when they embrace each-one-teach-one (a core Mindset practice) as a way of life? How much can you, your own and other countries and communities benefit from these teachings?

As I have stated, I wish to honour Nelson Mandela and his compatriots, and give others a chance to emulate their genius. To achieve this, I want this indigenous wisdom from South African history to be easier to replicate. I believe that as soon as you start to consider the foregoing questions, your thoughts and how you use your senses will contribute to your success in these endeavours. Specific examples and exercises that are most helpful are detailed throughout the book, mainly in Chapter 6.

Finally, I ask that you **dream** for a moment – about what you could achieve if you understood and applied the philosophies and practices that equipped Nelson Mandela to grow from rural herd boy to world-famous political prisoner, to internationally admired president of his country and winner of the Nobel Peace Prize. Anthony Sampson wrote, in a footnote to his *Mandela – The Authorised Biography*, 'When I was writing a book about the trial, *The Treason Cage*, I included profiles of Luthuli, Sisulu and

Introduction

Tambo, but not Mandela; I thought he was too detached to be a future leader, and would be less forthcoming.' (p. 107)

Imagine how successful you can be, whether at work, at home or in public, when you apply the MadibaMindset.

1

Why do it?

*Ubuntu is to do with one's humanity
being enriched by another's.*
NELSON MANDELA
In the Words of Nelson Mandela (p. 151)

MANY OF US SEEM UNABLE to do things we want to do and need to do, fully and completely. We tend to feel dissatisfied with our lot or our progress. Who or what should we blame? Maybe someone or circumstances are against us; or maybe it's because there is too much else going on over which we have no control and which frustrates what we want to do. Possibly we lack the necessary skills, finance or resources; or we lack the necessary mental or physical energy; maybe it's because we are unable to negotiate better.

We can easily create this experience because we know what we don't want, and not what we do.

Nelson Mandela served 27 years of a life sentence for treason. His conviction followed his dedication, from an early age, to the struggle. The struggle in South Africa started with a desire by the majority of South Africans to rid the country of the segregation system that was apartheid. When the South African government was initially ready to free Nelson Mandela he refused to go because **he** wasn't ready!

On the other hand, we 'normal' people continually grab at little bits of freedom and stay locked up in a prison of our own making. Why is that? Because, like most prisoners, we do what we are told to do, without understanding fully what matters to us. This is why so many of us know instinctively what we are against, without having any idea of what we are for. To some extent the cause of knowing clearly what we are against is rooted in normal childhood development. As children grow physically and develop emotionally, it is natural for them to rebel against all forms of authority – only the degree of rebellion and how it is expressed seem to vary. The young need to discover their own paths in life. As we grow older, we easily remember how we rebelled against figures of authority, like parents and teachers, and their path for our success. What we forget, or more likely never realise, is that this childhood rebellion is very often why we so easily recognise what we are against and struggle to uncover what we are for.

Thus a problem arises every time we allow our 'against' to outweigh our 'for', reducing our chances of success. This happens because being against something tends to be reactive or destructive, whereas being for something means being proactive or creative. And it is creation, not destruction, that leads to ongoing success. On some level, rational or emotional, every unproductive 'against' that we embody helps us to perceive another bar to our freedom. On the other hand, every time we know our 'for', we see past the bars of our self-constructed prisons. Ahmed Kathrada, an esteemed Robben Island graduate, said: 'Someone has written about two prisoners looking out of their cell window: one saw iron bars and the other stars.'

Remember Martin Luther King. He too spoke of the power of a **dream**. Train yourself to dream:

> As you sit quietly ... begin to let your thoughts be calmer ... and quietly imagine that you are inside ... a cell ... slightly wider than the length of your body ... as you look up you can begin to visualise ... what's outside the little barred window ... you can see much more than the bars ... use your imagination and start thinking about the MadibaMindset ... and so you are starting now and have begun your transformation to a more effective, enjoyable and meaningful life.

Once we have this awareness and open-mindedness, our approach to life can change exponentially. The options and opportunities that start to manifest using this new mindset can liberate and free

Why do it?

us from our 'against', and our inhibiting old habits. Our purpose and aims can be addressed with increased insight and knowledge; we will be able to apply our minds to challenges in ways that were not perceptible before. We can be stimulated to be more resourceful when we apply the tools of the MadibaMindset.

Undoubtedly, Mandela was against the metal bars of his cell, but that did not stop him from believing in what he was for. Even more, the bars did not stop him planning and plotting and preparing for what he stood for, and had committed his life to, every day for 27 years, so that he was ready to be president on the day of his release. That is the power of the MadibaMindset.

There are exercises in and at the end of the chapter to help you start practising the Mindset. As I have suggested and will explain more fully in Chapter 4, it can often start with a **dream**.

Knowledge is freely available these days – in books, in public libraries and on the Internet. We have easy access to the many examples of how other people achieved success, beat amazing odds, or survived in terrible situations. Examples of people who remained convicted and would not give up range from political leaders (such as Mahatma Gandhi and Aung San Suu Kyi) to death camp survivors (Viktor Frankl and Aleksandr Solzhenitsyn), and to relatively ordinary people, such as business entrepreneurs and others like Roxana Saberi and Sidney Poitier. Yet we often seem unable to apply the relevant knowledge and habits that these role models have willingly shared. Why?

Perhaps knowledge is not enough? Maybe we grew up with the convention that knowledge is power and that knowledge is the secret to success. Today we have ample evidence to realise that knowledge on its own is not enough. If you want to change, to lose weight for example, you can easily find information and knowledge about how to diet and exercise. But will that be sufficient to make a difference? Will simply knowing how create the desired outcome? Consider another really simple example. What should you do to save money and not have any debts? We all know the solution – spend less than you earn. Yet many struggle daily to apply this solution. **Knowing isn't enough** and that is why it is essential to **do the exercises** in this book.

Consider the following examples, and keep in mind that it takes wisdom to know when others are wrong and guts to go against what they want. Many years ago Henry Ford had the foresight to know how the newly created car market could evolve, and the guts not to listen to his customers. As he once pointed out, if he had listened to his customers he would have built a better horse and buggy. Henry Ford annoyed his fellow industrialists by doubling the pay of his factory workers. History has shown that Henry Ford was no fool when it came to producing high volumes at low cost. Yet, according to the conventional wisdom of the time, he was a total fool for willingly increasing his labour costs. What was he thinking? He was clever and realised that there was no point in building so many cars if so few people could afford them. He simply wanted his workers to be able to buy the cars they were making! And so the modern car era was born. That is the power of knowledge with conviction.

It is highly unlikely that Amazon.com, the Internet bookseller turned Internet retail giant, could exist today – never mind be so successful – without the trailblazing of Fedex's Fred Smith. He believed he knew why customers did not ask for an overnight package delivery service – because they had never before imagined it was possible. Based on this belief, Smith started FedEx and, by default, made the selling of products online possible. FedEx was not an overnight success. In fact, FedEx struggled through years of legal, financial and operational crises that threatened its survival. What kept FedEx afloat was the commitment and resourcefulness of its leaders and employees. For example, to survive recurring cash-flow problems in the early years, FedEx pilots often used their personal credit cards to pay for gas for their planes, and employees did not always cash their pay cheques. Once Fred Smith gambled the company's last remaining funds on blackjack in Las Vegas and won enough to keep the planes flying and to help meet a payroll. What kept them believing and kept them at it? Smith explained in one interview that he knew the idea was profound and that there was no doubt in his mind about that. His idea, knowledge, was backed up by his conviction, and executed with determination.

Roxana Saberi is an Iranian–American journalist who spent four months in an Iranian prison after being arrested in Iran in January 2009 on espionage charges, charges which she has denied. She was originally sentenced to eight years in prison. In an interview after her release she explained that she had been held with women political

Why do it?

prisoners who helped her to stay strong in prison. These women were already suffering the consequences of serving time in an Iranian prison and yet they told her that she should stand up for what she believed in, her convictions, even if that meant that she would stay in prison much longer. They urged her to tell the truth, even if she had to suffer for it.

Sidney Poitier is a Bahamian–American actor, film director, author and diplomat who became, in 1963, the first black person to win an Academy Award for Best Actor. In his book, *The Measure of a Man*, he writes about conviction. He explains that sometimes our convictions can cost more than we are willing to pay. He believes that irrevocable change may not occur when we are not up to paying the necessary cost, and can happen when we are. Either way, he argues, we must live with the consequences. Milton Erickson, the late American psychiatrist, is reputed to have said that 'you can have whatever you want as long as you pay ... attention to what is important. And if you don't pay attention ... to what is important ... you will pay with pain.'

The individuals in the examples above were entirely convinced about what they wanted to do. This generated a massive and determined effort to achieve their purpose in life. On the other hand, knowing without conviction is unlikely to lead to change or a mindshift. Perhaps you can think of examples of people you have actually met who are closer and more meaningful to you – be they family, friends or acquaintances – who have touched you and influenced you through their example of living with conviction. Can you remember how the way they dealt with something in their life impressed you, and perhaps how you tried their methods to deal effectively with similar situations in your life? Thinking about these closer-to-home individuals can be a powerful motivation, which is why we encourage you to prepare for the exercise at the end of this chapter as you **dream** again now:

> Start by sitting quietly ... become aware of your breathing ... slow it down and lengthen your out breath ... calm your mind as you start relaxing ... think about those people who have influenced your life, or those who you want to model ... consider the MadibaMindset ... recall the names

of those significant others ... recall what they did that was so important and how ... can you remember any associated feelings ... remember any insight that you recognised at the time ... remember how you felt, and if and how you resolved to use the same insights ... any of the same enriching attitudes and behaviours. Can you remember certain occasions when you felt successful after having applied their ways? Were these occasions noticeably different from how you used to deal with situations? ... Get ready to write down how you did things differently; write down the positive result achieved in this way and how you can apply these actions more frequently and on a daily basis.

Many of us have dreams and wish that we could change our current situation, improve it somehow and have a better life. We set goals for ourselves because we already know that unless we have a plan, unless we measure our progress against that plan and unless we learn to improve, we will not change anything for the better. Unfortunately, some of us have no goals and many do not achieve their goals, for whatever reason. Not achieving our goals to create the outcome we want is a common human condition. This is why over the ages many different methods have been developed to help us to stick to our resolutions and achieve our goals. Nevertheless, many of us remain frustrated with our lack of progress, embarrassed by our failures and exhausted by unrewarded effort. Our self-esteem suffers as we lose confidence in our abilities. It does not have to be that way. We can be different! The MadibaMindset enables you to clarify your conviction so that you can **apply your knowledge to your purpose**.

Sometimes people do not achieve their goals, despite commitment and application. Often this is because their strategy is inappropriate to their circumstances. Most highly visible strategies appear as if they are not designed for trying and restrictive conditions, whether actual or perceived. Rather, these methods presuppose availability of abundant resources that are often not immediately available or, even if they are, become unnecessarily squandered and can rather be saved for the future. When Paul Hawken received an honorary doctorate at Portland University in 2009, he said, 'We have tens of thousands of abandoned homes without people and tens of thousands of abandoned people without homes ... we are stealing the future, and selling it in the present, and calling it Gross Domestic Product ... we are vastly interconnected ... who will programme this civilisation's New Operating System?'

Remember from the Introduction that what transpired on Robben Island during the last decades of the twentieth century is the best example of how to turn a destructive system into a productive experience. The Robben Island experience shows clearly that it is possible to create a better future even as we find ourselves in systems – whether business, social, relationships and so on – which by design or default, dissipate emotional energy and restrict access to money and other 'necessary' tangible resources.

The MadibaMindset sets out the strategies used on Robben Island and in other restrictive situations, and teaches how these behaviours can be modelled to achieve more with less. This is a necessity for the restructuring of the world economy and future economic growth into the foreseeable future. It includes practical methods to enable you to turn your dreams into outcomes, even under trying and restrictive conditions. With trying and restrictive conditions as the probable underlying context, I suggest the following five good reasons to use the MadibaMindset.

1. We can achieve more and become more successful. We want a more successful life ... however we define success. Maybe we feel we can do more ... or do better. Maybe we feel stuck. Or maybe we don't know ... what we want to achieve ... in our lives ... in our careers ... or at home. The MadibaMindset can help us find positive purpose in our lives.

One of the key reasons that we often get stuck is because we are trapped in a mental prison. This mental prison can be of our own making – for example, our beliefs – or it can be as a result of peer pressure, advertising, media or other subtle forms of mind manipulation. The problem is that we are mostly **unaware of these mental prisons**. We might believe that we have free will and yet we think, feel and behave as others – parents, partners, friends and authority figures – want us to. As Aldous Huxley explains in his *Brave New World Revisited*, 'It is perfectly possible for a man to be out of prison, and yet not free – to be under no physical constraint and yet to be a psychological captive, compelled to think, feel and act as the representatives of the national state, or of some private interest within the nation, wants him to think, feel and act.' (p. 114)

Often the first step is simply to become aware of our mental prison. Only then can we realise that we have the key to the lock to set ourselves free. Surely, Nelson Mandela was very aware of the dangers of succumbing to a mental prison while locked up in a physical prison. I believe that the essential elements, which I call the 'core' of the MadibaMindset (described in Chapter 2), provide a structure to escape from these dangers!

Undoubtedly the Mindset can help us to improve both the results we achieve and our life experiences, because it is designed to liberate our minds, enhance our lives and increase our productivity. As said and quoted more fully later by an esteemed Robben Island graduate: 'It allowed people to develop an understanding that they could make a difference. It opened up the potential for ingenuity and self-organisation.'

2. We can overcome a lack of resources – both real and imaginary, whether in the form of time, money, energy or knowledge. The perilous state of the world economy and the health of the planet have highlighted just how wasteful current business and corporate practices have become in the utilisation of capital, human energy and natural resources. This has happened in spite of the call, for many years now, from business and economic thought-leaders, that we need to do more with less.

Today, success requires a better use of finite resources such as time, energy and money. This means we must focus on how we can deliver the outcome we want, and not be sidetracked by distractions. We must be clear about what we want, understand what matters most and has meaning to us. Be disciplined in application and action, learn to improve, and let go of what does not serve us or our purpose.

Mandela once said that it was essential to **forgive** his oppressors, because otherwise he could never achieve freedom from their influence. Scarce resources are simply oppressors trying to prevent you from achieving your goals and ultimate success. In this sense, scarce resources will strengthen our mental prison unless we find a way of forgiving them, of breaking free from their influence. One way of breaking free is to discard the inappropriate practices of the past

– the practices that no longer serve us effectively – and to embrace new ways.

By helping us to forgive our oppressors, the MadibaMindset can show us how to accelerate our self-empowerment progress regardless of resources at our disposal.

3. We can stay focused when we want to achieve a specific goal. We have made our resolution or set our goal. How can we make it happen? The first part is easy; the second is less so. Why? Although we have thought of a resolution and set a goal for the future, we may still be stuck in the past. The reason we remain stuck in the past is usually **habit**. We form habits because we learn from experience. If our experience has been how difficult it is to achieve our goals, rather than to resourcefully achieve them repeatedly, then we may believe that this is just 'the story of our life'.

Just because we have struggled to date is no guarantee that we will struggle tomorrow. The MadibaMindset will show us how to transform our history and capitalise on our accumulated experiences. As we gain confidence in ourselves and our abilities, we will find it easier to embrace flexibility and change our habits. We can replace destructive habits with habits that facilitate our success. Furthermore, the world changes constantly and it helps to keep up. Our history is both likely and unlikely to repeat itself, depending on what we do and the context of our lives. Our history will only repeat if our habits make it so, and recorded history often only resembles the past.

4. We can save time and effort by learning from the success of others. Some people like to do things on their own, even if it takes longer and brings more pain. Others prefer to save time, effort and pain, and so they use a coach or a programme like the MadibaMindset. We can achieve much more with much less if we are willing to learn from others who went before. Those thought pioneers who developed behavioural frameworks that work have already identified solutions to many common challenges along the way to success. Learn from them whenever you can.

It is very common, entirely acceptable and usually legal to create a better product by taking an existing one apart, analysing its workings in detail, and then to create a brand new product based on what an existing product does without infringing copyright. This process has a formal name: reverse engineering. One of the most famous examples of reverse engineering resulted in something as basic and practical as a gasoline container. By 1939 the Germans had manufactured a stockpile of cans in anticipation of World War II. The British and American forces noticed the excellent design of these gasoline cans and realised that the Allies had nothing equivalent. They promptly reverse engineered these cans and improved on the original. Hence the name we still use today: jerrycans. Today reverse engineering is very common in manufacturing. For example, car manufacturers deconstruct new models from competitors.

One interesting aspect of reverse engineering is that it starts with the desired outcome, such as a product or performance criterion. Then the engineer works backwards to uncover the design or actions required to create the desired outcome. The principles of reverse engineering apply equally to creating a better future in accordance with the ubuntu quotation heading this chapter. There are two basic ways of using reverse engineering to model personal behaviour in order to create better outcomes or success. You can start with a desired outcome and dream and deconstruct it, then work backwards to determine the steps you should take to achieve your desired outcome. Or you can learn from what other people have done to achieve success – record the steps they took, and then follow them precisely like a recipe. Napoleon Hill's *Think and Grow Rich* is probably one of the earliest self-improvement recipe books, preceded only by the famous historic spiritual texts.

5. We can develop and expand our leadership skills. The ability to craft a personal vision and then to live accordingly with conviction is a common trait of successful and fulfilled individuals. The ability to craft a business vision and strategy, and then to translate it into executable action steps, is a desirable leadership trait. Furthermore, knowing how to achieve goals with limited resources under trying circumstances is a critical and desirable skill with a wide range of potential applications.

There are many articles and books that attempt to analyse and explain Nelson Mandela's leadership style and characteristics. (One of the best articles was written by Richard Stengel who collaborated with Nelson Mandela on Mandela's bestselling autobiography *Long Walk to Freedom*. The article in question appeared on Time.com in July 2008 and is called *Mandela: His 8 Lessons of Leadership*.)

Mandela's leadership success is not only due to his unique leadership abilities. What sets Mandela apart is how he went about being a leader. He made it clear what he stood for and, by example, **he behaved in accordance with his convictions**. This habit is continually and consistently inspiring and is evident throughout his life story. The MadibaMindset is a recipe to follow and enables us to emulate some of his example.

Why did they do it?

We can gain a lot by considering why the Robben Island graduates did what is described in the following chapters. An important reason why they did it, and why we should do it, concerns keeping the spirit strong. The prisoners on Robben Island desperately needed some way to stay focused on their goal and not to give in to despair. Few situations are as demeaning and restrictive as being a prisoner. A great part of what makes us human is our ability to influence our situation and surroundings through the choices we make. In most situations we are free to decide on some course of action; we have some modicum of control.

Hardly so in prison – a prison is designed to allow inmates neither control nor freedom to decide on a course of action. Mandela and his fellow prisoners on Robben Island developed strategies that gave them control and emphasised behavioural choice. However, it takes a strong spirit and strong convictions to constantly control your thoughts and to consistently choose your reactions wisely.

In the words of Nelson Mandela in *Long Walk to Freedom*: 'I have found that one can bear the unbearable if one can keep one's spirits strong even when one's body is being tested. Strong convictions are the secret of surviving deprivation; your spirit can be full even when your stomach is empty.' (p. 363)

Another important reason why they did it was so that all that went before, all the suffering, would not be wasted. They realised that the time in prison could be used to prepare for when things changed in their favour. To some extent, Mandela's philosophy in prison can be summarised as follows:

- Success comes when we have had sufficient time to prepare.
- Use the time in prison wisely, as a preparation for the future.

- Understand what you can do now to start the process of creating your success.
- Live knowing that you will succeed; it is only a matter of time.
- Recognise that your current state or situation is simply a university to prepare you for duties and responsibilities that will come with your success.

Now let's consider and perhaps identify with rationalisations that arise when we don't feel we have a choice. Maybe they are part of why we choose not to do something.

- Because I am used to others telling me what to do – like bosses, systems, and procedures.
- Because I trip over myself, but I don't realise or accept that I get in my own way.
- Because I am not living my life, but someone else's idea of what it should be.
- Because, although I know what I am against, I don't know what I am for.
- Because I am a prisoner of the way I run my mind.

As you identify with any of the above, can you specify a first step toward change? If so, write it down now – if not, later chapters will help you start. The MadibaMindset is purposefully hardcore how-I-can-do-it and do-it-yourself material. You should be convinced to carry on with the programme as laid out in following chapters now. Nevertheless, some readers may need more academic conviction before proceeding, and others will just be interested, for other reasons, to read Appendix A ('Aiming higher'). Depending on your motivation, I leave it to you to choose whether to do it now or later, when you reach the end of the book.

For me, following the MadibaMindset recipe does not always come naturally and easily. Nevertheless I have found that starting with small steps does produce pleasant results and that the little steps of personal growth, which can go on for life, are most rewarding and enjoyable.

You can't keep doing things the same way and expect different results. Einstein is reputed to have said that doing the same thing and expecting different results is a sign of insanity. Invariably, for us to be more successful, something or someone has to change. Understand that change, like a coin, has two sides. Most of us want things to change because we want things to be better – even when things are already good we know they can be even better. That's one side of the coin – we want things to change. The catch is that any change requires us to change as well. This is the flip side – we must **be willing to change**.

But what if we are not prepared to change? As the saying has it, if we always do what we always did, we'll always get what we always got. It's as straightforward as that. Let's now accept that we want to improve – then something must change. However, for every action there is, according to Newton, an equal and opposite reaction. The minute the change of effort, awareness, consciousness or mindshift begins, some other force may start to resist that change. When it comes to personal change, then that force may be a natural internal resistance to anything that threatens our comfort zone. This may surface as excuses, a wait-and-see attitude, passive–aggressive behaviour, procrastination, and so on. A high level of conviction, in alignment with our values, can overcome this force!

Nelson Mandela and his fellow political prisoners turned their incarceration into a positive experience at every opportunity. They influenced anyone and everyone – because they believed that anyone could be turned to their cause. In other words, they believed that they could be 'agents of change'. Perhaps, when Mandela made the statement about ubuntu at the beginning of this chapter, he was too humble to think about how great a model he is for human enrichment? Chapter 2 starts to explain examples from Robben Island that we can follow to experience the human enrichment he refers to.

If you always do what you always did, you'll always get what you always got.

Think out of the box

- Sit quietly for a moment … and begin to becalm your thoughts.

- Imagine you are locked up in a cell slightly wider than your body length.

- Look up and start to visualise what you can see out of the window, which is about one foot square in size.

- What can you see outside and beyond the metal bars?

- How far and how clearly do you manage to see beyond the bars?

- Using your imagination, start entering into the MadibaMindset, and so commence your transformation into a more effective and productive existence.

- Write down what you saw beyond the bars.

Why do it?

Pretend to know

- Sit quietly for a moment and begin to becalm your thoughts.

- Become aware of your breathing ... breathe slowly ... and lengthen your out breath.

- Relax and notice how your thoughts become calmer.

- Pretend for a moment that you already know the MadibaMindset and recall something important you have read about it ... or recall the quote at the start of this chapter.

- Apply this knowledge as you imagine ... what you want to do better. Now imagine how successful you can be ... at work ... at home or in public, whenever you apply it consistently.

- In doing this exercise, did any thought or idea, something positive, occur to you? This thought can become a resourceful obsession.

- So remember it ... write it down ... It may stimulate a mindshift.

- Write down any additional things that came to mind.

Who I can model

- Sit quietly for a moment ... and begin to becalm your thoughts.

- Think about the people you know (family, friends, teachers, bosses and so on) who have had a positive influence on you and your life.

- Write down the names of at least a few of these people.

- Under each name write down the main lesson (behaviour, habit, idea, etc.) that you learned from them.

- Write down how you learned it from them; for example, they explained or taught it to you or you observed them in action and modelled their behaviour.

- Now consider carefully where in your life you have already applied these lessons and the outcome or outcomes you can attribute to these lessons.

- Finally, write down where, today, you can better apply these lessons and become even more successful at what you do.

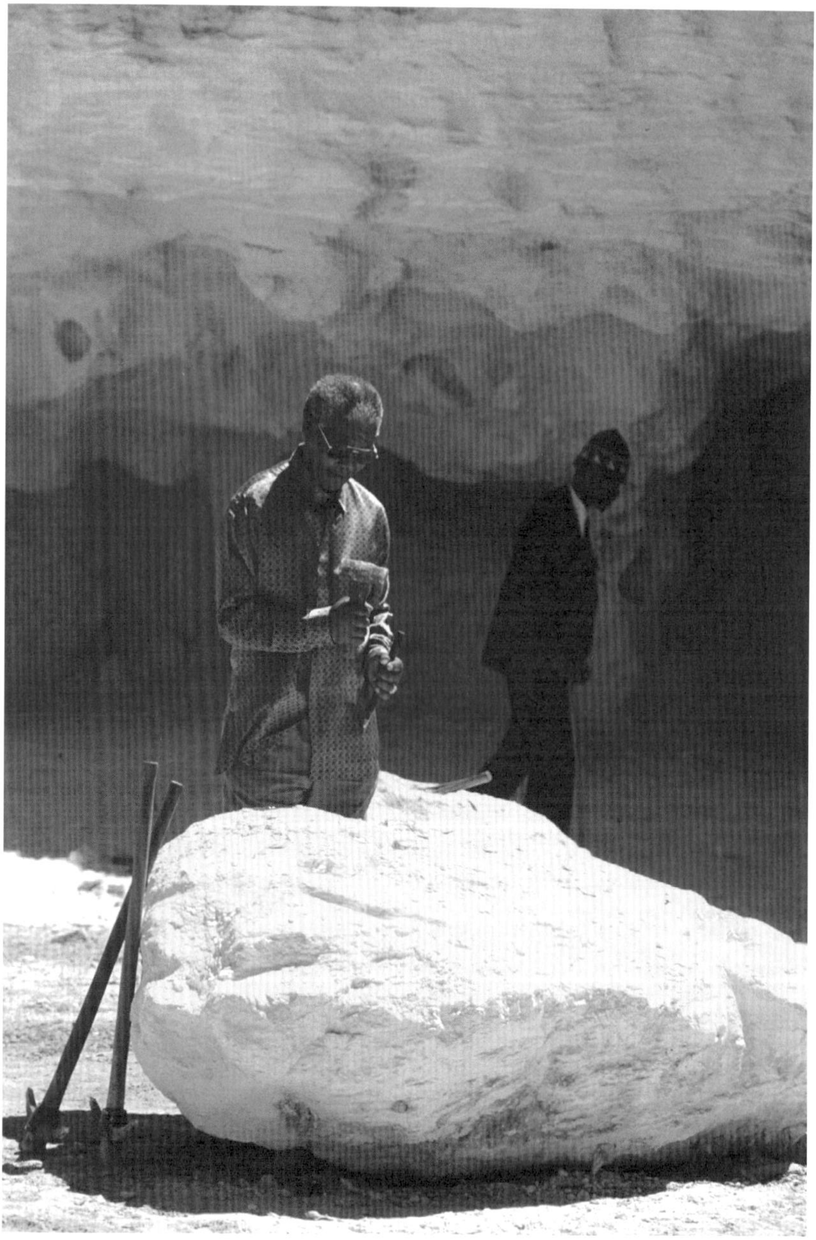

2

The core of the MadibaMindset

As unique as he might be, he would tell you that he is part of a long chain of Leadership.
RICHARD STENGEL
Mandela's Way (p. 229)

IN THIS CHAPTER I EXPLAIN my understanding of the core elements of the MadibaMindset. Again, I remind the reader that I am not a graduate of the Robben Island experience and that my description of these elements is incomplete and unofficial. I collected this information from an analysis of relevant in-depth reading and research, visits to Robben Island, and discussions with Robben Island graduates. My interpretation is certainly influenced by my study of what others have described about oppressive experiences. Furthermore, in my research I always had a filter to my thinking. This filter is the question: How can anyone **use this miracle as a personal self-development tool?**

I offer this interpretation with the conviction that when you apply some or all of the disciplines I describe here, then you will certainly improve both the results you achieve and your life experience. Mac Maharaj, himself a Robben Island graduate, captured the essence of what readers can model. In a newspaper article celebrating Mandela's 91st birthday, he wrote: 'The power achieved belongs not to some grand plan, but to the gathering of small efforts. It emerged from the growing sense that each effort was a little stream flowing into a mighty river. It allowed people to develop an understanding that they could make a difference. It opened up the potential for ingenuity and self-organisation.' (*Sunday Times*, 26 July 2009)

For the purposes of describing this model I have categorised the core of the MadibaMindset into the following five elements:

- Choose to look for the good in all situations and in all people before acting or reacting.
- Apply self-criticism before criticising as a means of empowerment.
- Continue to learn through the habitual use of each-one-teach-one.
- Perpetually enjoy mental and physical fitness.
- Consciously choose when to fight, flee or negotiate.

1. Look for the good
Look for the good in all situations and in all people before acting or reacting. An example of this core element is the manner in which the Robben Island graduates dealt with their prison guards. Regardless of what the guards did or how they behaved, the prisoners sought to connect with the humanity of the guards. A study of Mandela reveals that he deeply believes that all humans have a kernel of goodness within, and that we can make it our mission to discover it and work with it. Robben Island examples of this in action include the following:

- Prisoners made an effort to learn the Afrikaans language – the mother tongue of most of the prison guards – and converse with them in this medium. Afrikaners are proud of their heritage, of rising from oppression by the British. The Afrikaner nation is symbolised by their language. The respect shown to the guards earned reciprocal respect from them towards the prisoners, at times an acknowledgement that the prisoners also represented an African nation and an oppressed class. This established common ground between the guards and the prisoners, which is a foundational step in the building of rapport.
- The prisoners sorely missed relating to children who are, in their respective cultures as in most others, highly valued and enjoyed in community relationships. They sought to speak to the guards about their children, which gave them an opportunity to connect indirectly with children and to reach the guards' softer sides. This

is an almost universal reaction when both friend and foe enter the world of children together.
- Many of the prisoners were better educated and more literate than the guards. The prisoners encouraged the guards to further their education and were happy to assist them in their efforts. This helped the guards to appreciate that, although the prisoners were committed to overthrowing their captors' government, they had nothing personal against the guards themselves. They did not wish to limit the guards' lives in any way. Rather, they wished to initiate a process of growing together through mutual assistance. This created a foundation for mutual trust and respect as well as a fertile field for future achievement.

Use the first exercise at the end of this chapter to apply a similar approach to the way we behave. The exercise starts with a suggestion to empower our attitude towards others by habituating some simple steps. The exercise starts by suggesting you calm your thoughts. This is often easier said than done. To be calmer you can follow the specific procedure set out in Chapter 6. When you start using this new habit your rational mind can ensure that your emotions do not rule. Regardless, you will connect more easily and closely with others.

2. Apply self-criticism

Apply self-criticism before criticising as a means of empowerment. How consistently, when life does not turn out as we want it to, do we look for something or someone else to blame and so ensure that we render ourselves powerless? Counterintuitively, the MadibaMindset demands that in such circumstances **you first look at your own behaviour** before searching for a way to change it to a more resourceful pattern. An extremely useful question to ask yourself is: What can **I** do, regardless of what others are doing or will think, to change this situation either actually or experientially?

The inherent power in this question is that, whatever the circumstances, you can keep control of your own behaviour and therefore remain empowered. When you have considered all of the elements of the core of the MadibaMindset you will realise that all are strategies which can be followed regardless of what others are doing. In this context Derrick Grootboom, one of the Robben Island graduates, described self-criticism before criticising as follows: 'To have an open mind, to be brutally honest with yourself about what you do, to listen to critique, to constantly learn, to improve your skills, to be innovative in terms of constantly looking for new ways of achieving your goal – never be dogmatic (a word we always tried to avoid as a description of ourselves).'

It is easy to blame something else. Yet, it is clear, as soon as you fully and rationally consider this blame habit – from an observer's point of view – that it is totally disempowering. It enables you to become a prisoner of your own mind. In the context of Robben Island imprisonment, you can quickly and easily realise how simple and natural it would have been to blame the authorities for the entire situation. This was exactly what the government wanted because such a mindset would have allowed their regime to remain the custodian of all the power as well. Self-criticism therefore diluted the power of the captors and, over time, increased the ability of the prisoners to influence the outcome of their convictions.

The effectiveness of self-criticism is visible all over in the lives of successful people as soon as you open your eyes to its existence. I once enjoyed an enlightening outing on a beautiful boat with a successful businessman who was also the captain for the day. The captain was not as experienced in matters marine as he was in matters of international business, and had some difficulties operating the electronic navigation. On returning to the dock he requested that he be left in peace to study how the system worked. He commented that 'whenever something is not working how you want it to, the first thing to do is to check how you can change what you are doing, in order to have a better chance of making it work how you want it to'. The relevant exercise at the end of this chapter sets out how you can enable yourself to make this mindshift towards self-empowerment.

3. Continue to learn
Continue to learn through the habitual use of each-one-teach-one. We can easily appreciate in a world of alarming growth of population and unemployment – maybe after you use self-criticism – that continuous skills development and learning are essential to survive, and probably the only way to thrive in our highly competitive world. The Robben

Island graduates were a self-appointed government-in-waiting and you can work out what question led them to believe that:

- They had the time to learn the skills they would need, and did not have, to run the country once they were released. Previously their focus was on being freedom fighters and now they needed new skills to be able to govern.
- They had the 'luxury', via the duration of their prison sentences, of all the time they needed to study to achieve these skills.
- They were able to make Robben Island their university and so be far more productive in the context of the apparently limited resources available to them.

Although some of the prisoners were uneducated, many of them had high-level qualifications, including some who were teachers and lawyers. By practising self-honesty and humility it became apparent that most had some skill or knowledge that they could pass on to a fellow prisoner, no matter what his level of education was. Therefore, via a process of **skills transfer** and mutual mentoring, all could learn new skills. This empowered them to use their time productively towards the achievement of both personal development and their mutual greater goal.

This process of each-one-teach-one was carried out whenever and wherever possible. One of the best examples took place during the daily work squads in the lime quarry where many were employed cutting stones. The legend has it that when the guards were looking the other away subjects such as Maths and languages were taught simultaneously with achievement of the required stone-cutting quota. Teacher and student would pair together and a stick was used to write on the ground, an improvised chalkboard, where the subject was illustrated and learning exercises were completed. This is but one example of how knowledge was spread among the prisoners and Robben Island was turned into a university.

Later, after continued requests to the authorities and international pressure, permission was granted to study via correspondence with respected outside institutions such as the University of South Africa (UNISA) and various correspondence colleges. Utilisation of the knowledge on the island continued synergistically with outside study as students were assigned a qualified prisoner as tutor. This both improved the learning experience and encouraged the strategy of utilisation of all available resources by ensuring they were deployed in the most productive context.

How often do you imprison yourself in the status quo by deceiving yourself that education can only be found in the sometimes prohibitively expensive formal system? You can now start to **apply each-one-teach-one** by becoming aware of the learning opportunities offered by those around you, and the pursuit of mutual skills transfer. In this way opportunities can become abundant and affordable. The challenge is to want to start and to decide how to start. A specific procedure of how to do this follows at the end of this chapter. It suggests a mutual exchange of skills that is not altogether necessary, as outlined below.

According to some reports, we learn and respond to 10 per cent of what we hear, 15 per cent of what we see, 20 per cent of what we see and hear, 40 per cent of what we discuss with others, 80 per cent of what we experience directly or practise, and 90 per cent of what we attempt to teach others. You can learn the most by teaching others! Although the accuracy of the foregoing has been questioned, I experienced it myself when I was a student. I became an Accountancy lecturer in an emergency and this was my most productive learning experience in four years at college. It follows that an outright 'skills gift/skills transfer' is actually each-one-teach-one with economic multiplier effects! The reason for this is that the 'teacher' is achieving the highest possible level of learning by assisting the student.

4. Perpetually enjoy mental and physical fitness

Mental fitness will surely follow the continuous and dedicated application of each-one-teach-one. Logic suggests that this process develops an enquiring mind that continuously searches for appropriate knowledge and new ways of doing things. Readings and research about the Robben Island inmates and the personal history of graduates after incarceration suggest that most followed this path. Mandela is a prime, although not the only, role model of this core element.

A potentially dangerous trap is to imprison a vibrant mind in an unfit body. This can easily lead to imbalances and a lack of congruence. A lazy body will use its own initiative to find excuses for

The core of the MadibaMindset

why it should not exercise. This is itself an example of self-deception. We can all find a way to exercise that we enjoy, so ensuring that our bodies remain healthy and lively. This allows our minds to enjoy the freedom and encouragement of a healthy and vibrant home.

Mandela's favourite way of exercising, before being incarcerated, was boxing. He found that boxing offered many benefits. He explained in his autobiography *Long Walk to Freedom*: 'In the ring, rank, age, colour, and wealth are irrelevant. When you are circling your opponent, probing his strengths and weaknesses, you are not thinking about his colour or social status. I never did any real fighting after I entered politics. My main interest was in training; I found the rigorous exercise to be an excellent outlet for tension and stress. After a strenuous workout, I felt both mentally and physically lighter. It was a way of losing myself in something that was not the struggle. After an evening's workout I would wake up the next morning feeling strong and refreshed, ready to take up the fight again.' (pp. 167–168)

How can you imagine liberating yourself unless you realise that your own exercise habit, as a matter of choice, allows you to enter a wonderful ring of freedom?

When he was on Robben Island Mandela was incarcerated in a tiny cell, which he could easily have used as an excuse to cancel his daily exercise habit. This did not happen and every day he arose early and ran on the spot in his cell. In this way he started the day with a healthy dose of exercise and continued to do so even after his release. As he grew older he changed the form to taking a good brisk walk. He therefore continued to find a way to exercise regularly and is reputed to have said that it is such an entrenched habit, like brushing his teeth and making his bed in the morning, that he cannot stop himself from doing it whatever his schedule and location. No doubt this contributed to his reaching a ripe old age despite his difficult and demanding life.

For some of us exercise comes naturally and easily so that it is no struggle at all. For those for whom it is something of a struggle I, who often need a reminder to exercise, offer the following:

- We are not all morning people. You might find different times of the day to be more convenient and suitable. Select your own best time and do it then.

- If you have a sedentary occupation or lifestyle, it is especially good to get up and stretch regularly to avoid stiffness of both the body and the mind.
- The worse shape we are in the more we benefit when we start an exercise habit.
- Physical exercise (including stretching) relaxes the body and also the mind. That is the two-for-one benefit of regular exercise.
- If you start telling yourself why you can't do it, replace that thought with one extolling the benefits you can achieve from exercise.

Often it is merely our own 'mental prison' that prevents us from exercising. We can programme our minds to automatically choose to have an exercise routine and to be positive. **It is a mindshift!** The fourth procedure at the end of this chapter encourages us to base our exercise habits on something we enjoy. I have found that once a part of my body gets a little stronger and healthier I start to take an interest – 'dream' about doing something mental and physical to stimulate the rest.

5. Consciously choose when to fight, flee or negotiate

After the adoption of the Freedom Charter by the Congress of the People in 1955, the African National Congress (ANC) began in earnest to attempt negotiations with the South African minority government. The ANC's goal was a free, non-racial democracy, in alignment with the Freedom Charter, and embracing universal franchise. The efforts to negotiate were completely unsuccessful because the South African government was rigidly committed to a policy of separate development known as apartheid. The extent of this commitment to apartheid was backed up by Afrikaner church leaders who managed to interpret the Bible to show a biblical justification for separate development.

Once it became clear that the minority government was not interested in negotiation, Mandela came to the forefront, being innovative in terms of looking at new ways of achieving the ANC's goals. This led to a decision by the ANC to act on two fronts:

- The armed struggle was initiated with the specific purpose of attacking strategic installations such as power stations. The plan

was to fight by causing damage to the economy and so encourage the government to reconsider.
- There was a flight by certain key ANC members to foreign lands where they could receive military and other training. Most importantly, this created the opportunity to change the context of the struggle through international public relations efforts. This strategy totally discredited the apartheid policy internationally. South Africa became so unpopular that it became the skunk of the world at the time. One of the benefits of this strategy was that Mandela and the ANC gained a huge amount of recognition and credibility.

This two-pronged approach of fight and flight took a long time to convince the authorities that the country had become 'ungovernable' on the basis of apartheid ideology. In addition, the various Afrikaner churches did an about face and decided that apartheid was a sin against humanity. Although this led to the realisation that apartheid had to end, it further exacerbated the fears of the white minority, which were triggered by the possible consequences of the demand for one-man-one-vote. This fear was the context of a stalemate towards the end of the apartheid disgrace. Although Mandela's political party remained committed to the aforementioned fight and flight, he started to **think more flexibly**:

'Like Homer's Odysseus he progressed from challenge to challenge, overcoming each one not because he was stronger than his foes but because he was cleverer and more beguiling. He had forged these qualities following his arrest and imprisonment in 1962 when he came to realise that the route of brute force he had attempted, as the founding commander of the ANC's military wing, could not work. In jail he judged that the way to kill apartheid was to persuade white people to kill it themselves, to join his team, submit to his leadership.'

This quotation is from the book *Playing the Enemy – Nelson Mandela and the Game That Made a Nation* (p. 17), now renamed *Invictus*, by John Carlin. It is an enthralling account of the opportunistic genius Madiba learned, enabling him to successfully conclude the world's only negotiated revolution. I recommend you read this book with a view to becoming able to model Mandela's strategies. Those who have read Malcolm Gladwell's *Outliers* and know the story will no doubt recognise the synergistic opportunities that Mandela recognised and utilised. Simultaneously, FW de Klerk, South Africa's last white president, was also realising it was time to negotiate.

After you consider the foregoing you can be convinced that, as Derrick Grootboom wrote, 'fight remains a last option and even if you fight you have to fight in such a way that you can still engage that person or warder as a fellow human being whom you have ultimately the goal of changing to your way of seeing things.' Later, this book will detail some specific strategies that explain how to do this. Because our emotions often take over, the sooner we can master these strategies the better. Should we not do this was be prone to get stuck in fight, and then later, maybe flee forever! Fight and flight are only temporary steps in a process and are sometimes unnecessary. As fight and flight often come naturally, the sooner we can make their adoption a choice, the better we are able to negotiate.

The South African negotiated revolution is unique in world history and led to one of the world's most respected constitutions. As we read and study more about how this was done, we can start to appreciate, understand and replicate the skills involved. A few examples to whet the appetite are:

- The ability to choose when and how to be precise, abstract or specifically vague are essential. Remember the one-man-one-vote demand and the fears it triggered for many white South Africans? Nobel Peace Prize winner FW de Klerk, who released Mandela from prison, told his followers that 'there will be a new system whereby everyone would have a vote of equal value' and reassured them that 'there would be checks and balances to ensure that oppression of the majority by the minority was not replaced by oppression of the minority by the majority'. With these words he stimulated thinking about how the new system would work and the new possibilities it opened up. This replaced the fear triggered by the old terminology 'one-man-one-vote', and so helped loosen the previous logjam. A referendum followed and, encouraged by the Afrikaner church leaders' about face on apartheid, it signalled support by the previously fear-paralysed minority for a new dispensation.

The core of the MadibaMindset

- During CODESA (Convention for a Democratic South Africa) there was a notoriously difficult stage when Mandela felt that he had been tricked by De Klerk into giving him, De Klerk, the last political word in the schedule of speakers concerning important principles. Mandela was undoubtedly angry and it was suspected that he remained hostile. Afterwards the press, sensing that Mandela could be about to stall the proceedings, pressed him on the issue. Somehow Mandela brought his sense of humour into play and responded to the questions by saying that 'the person who gets the last word is not necessarily the person who speaks last'.

The final exercise in this chapter enhances your ability to choose, and so initiate productive negotiation and resolution. Consider all the ideas presented here and in the exercises, so that you can be specific in now consciously choosing whether you will continue to fight, whether you will walk away – take flight – or whether you have created an opportunity to negotiate. Always make a note of your choice.

The question remains, to be answered in subsequent chapters: Why should I, and what will motivate me to?

Look for the good

- Sit quietly for a moment ... and begin to becalm your thoughts.

- Make a list of some of the people with whom you have important relationships.

- These people are often called significant others and include relationship partners, family members, friends, colleagues and your superiors at work. Review your list.

- Decide how you can specifically choose to look for the good in these significant others before acting or reacting.

- Now decide how you can specifically choose to look for the good in all situations before acting or reacting.

- Write down these specific methods. This way you can revisit your ideas and track their effectiveness and outcomes.

The core of the MadibaMindset

Criticism and self-criticism

- Sit quietly for a moment ... and begin to becalm your thoughts.

- Think of something that you find mildly irritating.

- Think about how you feel about it, what it means to you, how you react to it.

- Take a few deep breaths ... and breathe more slowly ... breathe in slowly ... and reread the last two paragraphs on page 29.

- With this in mind, ask yourself the question: What can I do, regardless of what others are doing or will think, to change this situation? Briefly write down your answer.

- How do you feel about it now? Differently? If so, write down how. Can you think why?

- If not, start again and repeat until you feel differently.

Each-one-teach-one

- Sit quietly for a moment after you calm your thoughts.

- Think about your skills. Which of your skills would you like to share with someone else?

- Who could that person be? Do you know someone who could benefit from your teaching and sharing?

- What skills does this person have that you want to learn? Are there other people who have skills that you would like to learn?

- How can you best approach them about this mutual exchange of knowledge and skill?

- Remember to apply the following: the goal is to find and actualise the opportunity that will be most beneficial to both parties.

Mental and physical fitness

- Sit quietly for a moment after you calm your thoughts.

- Think of an activity that you enjoy.

- Work out, and write down, how you can use this enjoyable activity to begin exercising and how to get into the habit of exercising regularly.

- Be specific in how you will start small and how you will then apply a process of continuous and incremental enhancement.

- Consider whether you need to incorporate each-one-teach-one as a way of getting started, and of keeping yourself motivated and committed.

Choose between fight, flight and negotiate

- Sit quietly for a moment after you calm your thoughts.

- Consider an important fight that you have not been able to resolve and may have run away from.

- Think of the benefits you can achieve by resolving this issue through negotiation, rather than through fight or flight. Write them down.

- Now consider how you can still choose to look for the good in this situation and in your 'opponent' before you act or react again.

- Next, consider whether you have applied self-criticism before criticising your 'opponent'.

- Explore whether the conflict might present an opportunity for mutual learning through each-one-teach-one.

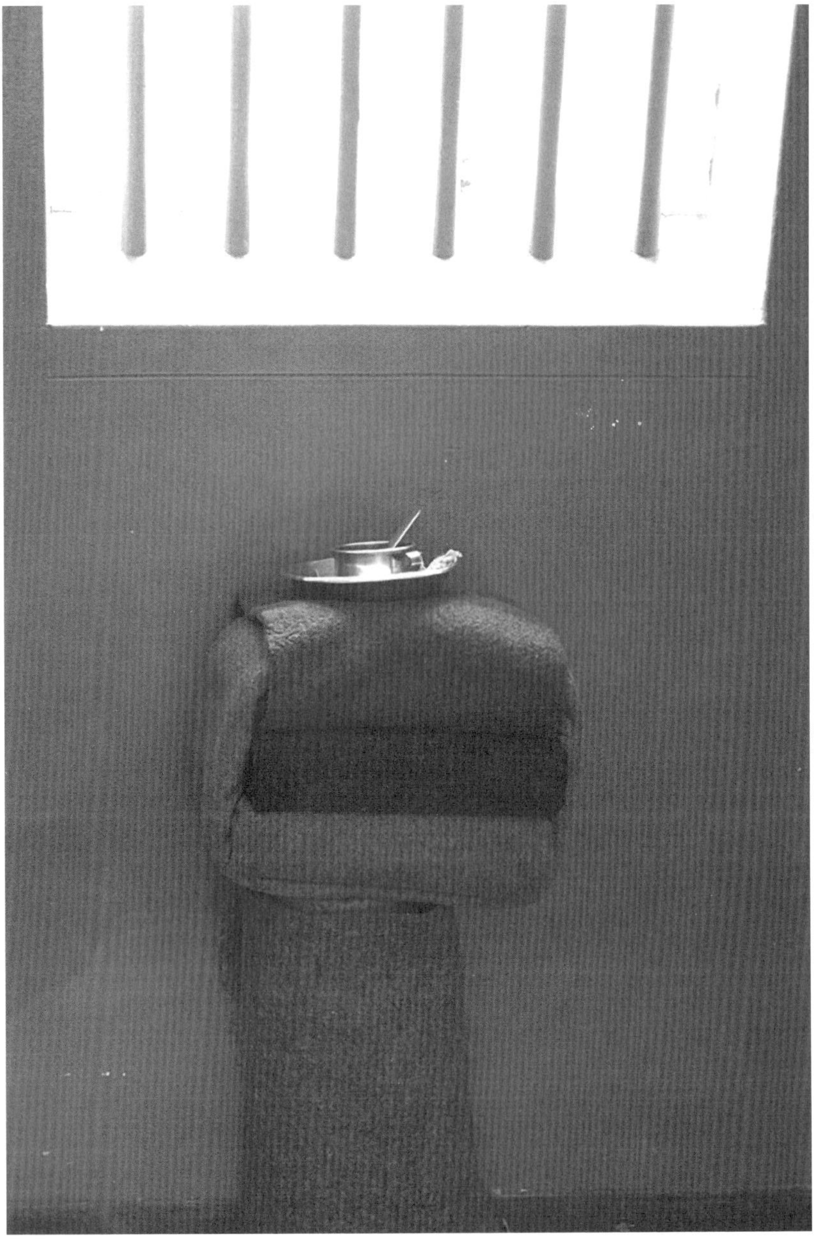

3

Conviction creates energy

There is nothing in content worth knowing without knowledge of contemporaneous relevant context.
NEUROLINGUISTIC PROGRAMMING (NLP) FUNDAMENTALISM

IT IS ESSENTIAL TO REMEMBER the five elements that comprise the core of this model of the MadibaMindset. These five elements are actually behavioural disciplines the Robben Island graduates practised and applied consistently. As Nelson Mandela and the other Robben Island graduates have demonstrated, these five disciplines are universal tools for great achievement. How did they manage to apply these disciplines so consistently in an environment designed to instil a different kind of discipline, one hostile to their constructive intentions? I believe that the answer lies in four foundational convictions that underpin and therefore empower the five disciplines. The four are: values, habits, strategies and structures:

- **Values:** The Robben Island graduates continued to live according to the values and beliefs that mattered to them on the outside – for example, that each human life has equal value. They did not succumb to the values and beliefs of the guards at the time: for example, that racial segregation was biblically justified and that white people are superior.
- **Habits:** In prison Nelson Mandela continued the positive habits, such as regular exercise, that he had developed on the outside.

By example he encouraged others to do the same. It also appears that the graduates adapted their habits or developed new ones to specifically counter the negative habits that the guards wanted them to adopt. For instance the political prisoners purposefully stood up straight to overcome the stoop that evolves from being forced to be subservient.

- **Strategies:** To continue their efforts towards the goals they had fought for on the outside, they revised existing outside strategies and created new inside strategies. Thus they modified their strategies to more closely match the new context, specifically to counter the inherent destructive and dehumanising purpose of the prison system.
- **Structures:** They adapted the outside organisational structures of the ANC and created new prison and cell structures. This enabled execution of their modified strategies, so countering the mind-numbing routines and restrictive structures of prison life.

Have you noticed that although the political prisoners on Robben Island adapted their habits, strategies and structure to their new environment, they did not waver from their conviction to their most important values? How clearly do we understand what I mean by values in this text?

Values

Some think that values and beliefs are the same. It is, however, important to realise that they are different and that the difference matters because values and beliefs influence behaviour in different ways. Beliefs are what we hold to be **true**, whereas values are what we hold to be **important**. Beliefs mainly determine our attitudes and opinions, whereas values mainly determine how we act on these attitudes and opinions. For example, a belief in the essential equality of human beings does not automatically translate into behaviours that demonstrate this belief in action. This is because beliefs tend to be more abstract in nature. A belief that all men are equal does not make it true. However, if you value this belief, then you can strive towards making it a reality in your sphere of influence.

Beliefs such as 'all men are born equal', often tend to be about things outside of our control'. Values can be self-defined and so tend to focus more on 'What can I do?' In the context of the foregoing you can write down the answers to the following questions as you apply your thoughts to the MadibaMindset – experience the difference between beliefs and values:

- What do I believe about the MadibaMindset?
- What do I value about the MadibaMindset?

Often beliefs are the assumptions we make about our model of the world; they usually comprise ideas or concepts that we accept as true, often without proof or evidence. As these are based on assumptions, beliefs can vary considerably from one person to the next.

On the other hand, values can be similar even if beliefs differ. For example, different religions may have different beliefs, but have many values in common. No doubt Nelson Mandela understood this, which is why he could look for the good – the values – in people who so obviously had different beliefs about the world.

To be able to respect other people's models of the world it is important that we accept the difference between values and beliefs. In addition we are more likely to be successful at what we want to achieve in life if we know the difference between what we value and what we believe. One reason for this is that our beliefs can easily change over time, as our assumptions are tested and questioned, whereas our values may not simultaneously change. Our beliefs about the world and our place in it may cause us to value leadership by example. We can change our beliefs as our understanding of how the world works changes. Perhaps new 'natural laws' are scientifically proven to apply, or new 'truths' become commonly accepted. Notwithstanding, it is unlikely that our new beliefs can reduce the value we place on leadership by example.

I tend to believe that we are more likely to be successful at what we want to achieve in life if we base our actions on what we value and not only on what we **believe**. This is because beliefs are individual assumptions, not necessarily shared by others, and can sometimes make rational thinking and discussion difficult, if not impossible. Furthermore, beliefs tend to stir up emotions, and emotions can hold us back from acting on our values. Emotions are terrific energy generators and it is therefore important to focus them on what is important.

Before I address in more detail why and how habits, strategies and structures tend to be adapted, I want to explain why context matters and how inflection points can unexpectedly change context. Context matters because we acquire beliefs and values through the context of our lives. Reflexively we perceive and interpret context our way, based on our unique life experience and in the context of the beliefs and values we have acquired and/or are developing.

The context of Mandela's life as a black village boy from a royal family sitting and listening to the wisdom 'of the purest form of democracy' in the Great Place of the regent probably stimulated his beliefs about the original good and equality of all humanity. Later, when he experienced the dogma of apartheid, another life context contradicted these beliefs – he undoubtedly experienced at least some degree of inner conflict as his beliefs were tested and his dignity was insulted. I believe that this experience stimulated values in Mandela, such as that it is extremely important that I do all I can to rid my country of this injustice to humanity and achieve freedom for my people! We can read about his youth, education, and professional and political life in the context of developing beliefs and values, as recorded in *Long Walk to Freedom* and other biographical literature. This reading can take on new meaning even if we have read the books before.

The opening quotation to this chapter implies that nothing occurs in a vacuum. No event, no action, no behaviour, no thought, no feeling – nothing – occurs in a vacuum. It is therefore critical that we know and understand, as best we can, the context within which we find ourselves. Otherwise it will not be easy to be successful. Why? Because it is **context that gives meaning** to events, actions, behaviours, thoughts, feelings and everything else. This is summarised in the following diagram. If you have already read *Long Walk to Freedom*, it is fascinating to review the book according to the structure of this diagram:

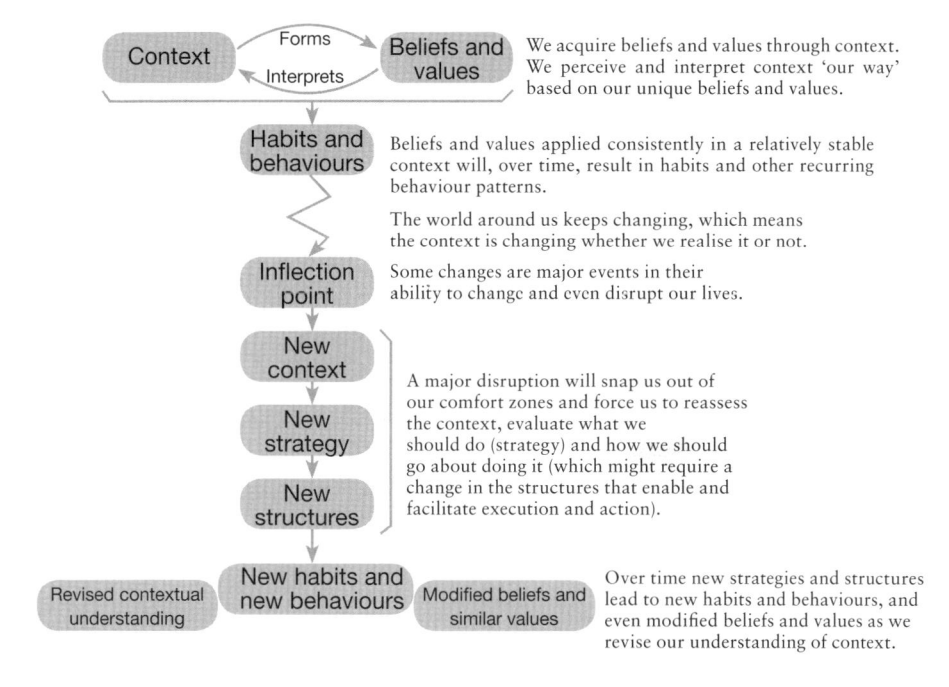

Conviction creates energy

Context ⇄ (Forms/Interprets) Beliefs and values		We acquire beliefs and values through context. We perceive and interpret context 'our way' based on our unique beliefs and values.
Habits and behaviours		Beliefs and values applied consistently in a relatively stable context will, over time, result in habits and other recurring behaviour patterns.
		The world around us keeps changing, which means the context is changing whether we realise it or not.
Inflection point		Some changes are major events in their ability to change and even disrupt our lives.
New context → New strategy → New structures		A major disruption will snap us out of our comfort zones and force us to reassess the context, evaluate what we should do (strategy) and how we should go about doing it (which might require a change in the structures that enable and facilitate execution and action).
Revised contextual understanding — New habits and new behaviours — Modified beliefs and similar values		Over time new strategies and structures lead to new habits and behaviours, and even modified beliefs and values as we revise our understanding of context.

When Mandela and his colleagues arrived on Robben Island they had to make sense of the new context within which they found themselves. They had to decide how they were going to experience the event/inflection point of being locked up for life. Were they going to live according to prison strategies and structures already in place, or could they adapt the strategies and structures of the ANC for life in prison?

We know that Mandela was sentenced to life imprisonment. The main purpose of a life sentence is generally to remove the prisoner permanently from society. Perhaps this is what Nelson Mandela's sentence was meant to achieve. There was no need to reform or rehabilitate him as he was never going to be released. The law may not have been concerned with how the sentence was executed. It is sufficient to say that history has shown that the conditions in which the political prisoners found themselves on Robben Island were based on strategies and structures designed to create everything other than freedom or comfort. It also appears certain that there was no intention to release anyone who remained convicted according to the values of the Freedom Charter.

Based on the philosophy of the Freedom Charter that the ANC

adopted in 1955, one can argue that its purpose, namely freedom for all people, was the exact opposite of that of the prison system. The context within which it operated was that the majority of the people of South Africa were not free. Hence, the strategies and structures that the ANC adopted were designed to achieve freedom. Keep in mind that apartheid South Africa was in many ways similar to a prison, especially for so-called non-white people who were physically confined to certain areas and deprived of a range of personal freedoms.

The fact that Nelson Mandela was released from serving a life sentence and the fact that the ANC changed from being against the people in power to being the people in power, shows how dramatically any context can change. Dramatic change of this nature has become known, at least in business, as a strategic inflection point.

In his book *Only the Paranoid Survive*, Andy Grove defines a strategic inflection point as a time when the fundamentals of a business are about to change. The change can create opportunities for some people and organisations to excel, while for others it can trigger the beginning of the end. You may find yourself at the receiving end of a strategic inflection point or you can be the cause of one. Inflection points take time, often years, to play out. You may realise in a flash of illumination what is going on around you. However, making the required behavioural changes and implementing your new plans can take months if not years.

Grove also explains that to get through an inflection point you need to remain objective, you must be willing to act on your convictions and you must somehow demonstrate your passion so that others will be mobilised into supporting those convictions. At the time of writing his book, Grove was the CEO of Intel Corporation. As president of Intel, he helped it get out of the memory chip business it was founded on, and to build a totally different world leader business based on microprocessors.

In the same way, the ANC got out of the 'business' of simply being against the government in power, and became an organisation that could articulate what it stood for – the strategic inflection point was the Congress of the People. Intel's strategic inflection point was triggered by its Japanese memory-chip competitors. The difference was that the ANC created and triggered an inflection point for the National Party regime. In August 1953, at the annual conference of the Cape region of the ANC, Professor ZK Matthews suggested the convening of a Congress of the People to draw up a Freedom Charter. Months in planning, the Congress of the People took place on 25 and 26 June 1955 at Kliptown, near Johannesburg. With hindsight, the adoption of the Freedom Charter at the Congress of the People can be seen as an inflection point because it changed the thinking of millions of people from what we are against – apartheid – to what we stand for, what we will fight for and in Nelson Mandela's case (and probably that of many other unnoticed heroes) 'what I am prepared to die for'.

Grove makes the point that because Intel responded forcefully, making a strong and definite decision, to the strategic inflection point, things turned out far better. The South African government responded forcefully, using brute physical force and the clout of newly enacted draconian laws, to the Congress of the People and its adoption of the Freedom Charter. This response to the inflection point triggered by the ANC appeared to be successful in the short term because it helped the National Party government stay in power for almost another four decades. Most people today know that this outcome was not a success. The Chinese government reacted similarly to Liu Xiaobo's Charter 08 and sentenced him on Christmas Day, after a two-hour trial, to 11 years for subversion. At his trial Liu said 'no force can block the human desire for freedom'. To the dismay of the Chinese government he was awarded the 2010 Nobel Peace Prize. How much more similar will these two stories look in the future?

Why is this discussion on strategic inflection points so important? Some readers may be doing so out of interest or a desire to make a few relatively minor changes in their lives. Others may be reading it because of a radical event, an inflection point, in their own lives, an event that has forced them to respond and to make drastic changes. I do not know how many readers may actually be ready to trigger an inflection point in their lives – where they make radical, yet positive, changes wilfully and with purpose. Inflection points force you to change your strategies and structures, your bad habits as well as habits that are now inappropriate. However, inflection points should not generally change your values. That is why you should be clear what your values are and thus what you stand for. One of the exercises you will do later in this book is to draw up your own freedom charter.

You may be aware that the Rivonia Trial and the subsequent life sentences imposed on Nelson Mandela and his comrades was another inflection point, this time created by the apartheid government and imposed on the various resistance movements and on specific individuals. This time they had to respond, and Mandela did so in his statement from the dock by staying true to his values: 'But if needs be, it is an ideal for which I am prepared to die.'

He did not die and when Mandela and his fellow prisoners arrived on Robben Island they had to make sense of the new context within which they found themselves. More than that, they had to respond objectively, tactically and practically to a new restrictive lifestyle in a way that would permit them to keep their values, modify their habits and at the same time reconcile them with their convictions, within the prison context. To a great extent, values and habits determine how you are likely to behave in prison, as well as in all other contexts – that is how you will react to the strategies and structures already in place.

Habits

Habits matter because, ultimately, our habits define our lives. Over the centuries wise men have warned us to watch our thoughts because thoughts precede actions, actions can become habits, and so our lives develop. We know little of what the Robben Island graduates thought and little of what they said in prison. Books like *Island in Chains* by Indres Naidoo (with whom I had the privilege of working) are extremely detailed in this regard. By reading and other research we can develop sufficient understanding of how their actions became habits. We also know the outcome – men and women of character who created, and then lived according to, their beliefs and values, at least in the Mandela years in South Africa.

Habits are acquired behaviour patterns that are repeated within context. When we behave in the same manner, repeatedly, in the same context, then over time this behavioural link between context and action becomes wired in – so that in a specific context, we tend to behave according to our habits. Good habits and bad habits are created the same way – by repeating the behaviour over and over until it happens without thinking about it, and it becomes unconscious or automatic. This means that we have the power to create positive habits as soon as we can institute a plan to repeat the desired behaviour often enough. We can also learn to more effortlessly create positive Pavlovian stimulus response patterns for ourselves.

Warren Buffet, celebrated for being the most successful investor the world has known, once said that 'bad habits are like chains that are too light to feel until they are too heavy to carry'. So always remember that there is nothing to stop us from putting them down, apart from our own mental conditioning or beliefs. John Wareham, author of *How to Break Out of Prison*, points out that all prisons are mental prisons. Mental prisons do not lock from the outside, but from the inside – we lock ourselves in. The inherent and necessary belief is that **we can let ourselves out by discarding limiting beliefs, when we want to.**

If habits tend to be linked to a specific context, what happens when the context changes? Often the change is not powerful enough to make us aware that our automatic behaviour has become obsolete and that we need to change our habit accordingly. When the change is startling enough, we react by either dropping the habit or adapting it. An example from Mandela's life is how he adapted his habit of regular exercise, picked up through his love of training as a boxer, to the confines of his cell. He continued to exercise for an hour every day. Yes, there was a deliberate motive to this habit of regular exercise. To the political prisoners on Robben Island, exercise and sport were important because they believed that on their release – graduation – they would become the government. Then an unfit graduate would become a burden, not an asset. All of the foregoing, and even many unwanted things, have now happened.

You cannot know what you don't want without thinking about it first! How then can we proactively drop bad habits and cultivate good habits because our subconscious senses do not process negatives? One way is to follow a strategy developed by Alcoholics Anonymous. The only requirement for membership of Alcoholics Anonymous is a desire to stop drinking alcohol. This creates the problem that you have to think about what you don't want to do in order to be a member. The subconscious does not remember negatives and that habits are run unconsciously. The organisation has overcome this problem by a brilliant suggestion that whenever you think about having a drink you just put off doing it till tomorrow. In other words, you practise positive procrastination. We can use positive procrastination to break a bad habit. However, this is only a first step because when we break a habit we create an activity vacuum that needs filling in order to maintain balance. The next question then becomes, what positive thing can I now do instead? In the context of creating an exercise habit, the appropriate steps can be:

- Decide how to do the type of exercise you want to habituate. Use each-one-teach-one for this if you want to.
- Catch yourself as you start thinking about or doing a bad habit you wish to discard. Put it off until tomorrow.
- Do the new exercise immediately – and if you think of not doing it, change the thought to the benefits you can achieve when you do it.
- Think again about the benefits you are after and continue to enjoy this thought when doing the replacement activity.

Always remember that positive procrastination is not enough. That's why even organisations such as Alcoholics Anonymous use strategies similar to those the political prisoners practised on Robben Island – each-one-teach-one, for example. Just like the Robben Island story, AA executes a strategy in the context of organisational beliefs, values and structures.

Strategy defines structure

Alfred Chandler began studying organisations in the early 1960s. He observed that the way an organisation was structured tended to be a response to the organisation's business strategy. Professor Chandler proposed that when a business adopted a new strategy it often needed to design a new organisational form to better execute the new strategy. Simplistically, organisational structure is the way managers coordinate and organise resources to implement strategies and execute plans. As strategies change and evolve, the organisational form needs to adapt as well. This insight has been popularised as 'structure follows strategy'.

We often forget that structure follows strategy, or sometimes we assume that our personal strategies don't require structure to facilitate their execution. We continue to use old tried-and-tested, worn-out structures and ways of doing things even as changes in the world around us demand that we adapt our personal strategies for success. And yet, as Mandela and his fellow prisoners demonstrated, **we are always able to have some measure of control over the strategies and structure we adopt.** The political prisoners on Robben Island did not adopt strategies according to the prison structures. They designed strategies according to what they wanted to achieve. They adapted the strategies they used outside to conditions inside, and then adapted the structures they had used outside for conditions inside. The following extract from his autobiography, *Long Walk to Freedom*, shows just how well Mandela understood the need to adapt his and the ANC's strategies and structures to the prison context:

'One must know the enemy's purpose before adopting a strategy to undermine it. Prison is designed to break one's spirit and destroy one's resolve... I was in a different and smaller arena, an arena for whom the only audience was ourselves and our oppressors. We regarded the struggle in prison as a microcosm of the struggle as a whole. We would fight inside as we had fought outside. The racism and repression were the same; I would simply have to fight on different terms.' (pp. 340–341)

The dream remained the same, and their beliefs and values convinced them victory was certain. Once convicted, their short-term goals were how to survive incarceration and be ready to take power. When released, they again had to adapt from being a government-in-waiting to one in power. Peter Schutz, a former chief executive officer of Porsche AG, once explained that during times of change and uncertainty, leaders must help their organisations to decide like a democracy and to implement like a dictatorship. It is better to have people arguing upfront while making a decision together, even if it takes time and even if the decision is flawed. Why? Because a decision that people support, even a flawed one, can be implemented quickly whereas a dictatorial decision, even if it is right, may not be executed at all. He also pointed out that most managers tend to do the opposite – they make autocratic decisions that are then bogged down in democratic implementation.

According to Mandela's own account, the decision-making process employed by the political prisoners was exactly that – lots of discussion upfront followed by focused action. In other words, they decided like a democracy and implemented like a dictatorship. I remind you here of what was explained in the introduction about Mandela's self-professed leadership style: 'As a leader, I have always followed the principles I first saw demonstrated by the regent at the Great Place. I have always endeavoured to listen to what each and every person in a discussion had to say before venturing my own opinion.' (*Long Walk to Freedom;* p. 19) It seems that Mandela always knew that no superstar can achieve anything without the help of ordinary people who are willing to defend and stand up for the same thing or cause. This is why he made sure that the necessary structures were in place to enable the support base of the ANC to rise to transcend extreme opposition.

How can we create democratic decision-making and autocratic action in our own lives? We can create an organisational structure around us that facilitates implementation and execution of our plans. When we have a dream and are developing a strategy or plan to achieve it, then surely we can organise all the resources at our disposal? As outlined above, we do need strategies and an action plan that keeps us on track towards achieving our dream or success. The rest of this book will help you to clarify your dream and define what success means to you, and what you stand for. You can then draw up your own freedom charter.

What if you already have an idea of what this is but you are unsure if it is right for you or you don't know how to turn it into appropriate strategies and actions? This is where creating organisational structure can help – create your own 'board of directors'. Napoleon Hill, who wrote many books in the early half of the twentieth century on 'how to get rich', called this group of people a 'Mastermind'.

Our 'Mastermind' comprises people we believe in, because we respect their experience and achievements. They can help us to think through our ideas and assist us to be accountable for our actions towards our goals. We can easily find out more about how to utilise our own Mastermind group by reading Napoleon Hill's books or by searching for the relevant information on the Internet. However, there are two important aspects we should keep in mind when considering our own group. As with a board of directors, we should meet with them regularly, individually or as a group. This means that the people we select must be willing to invest their time and effort in us. This brings us to another important point – few focused people are willing to, or can afford to do this without some return. Right from the start we must consider what benefit would be in it for them. Remember the practice of each-one-teach-one and consider what it is that we can offer them in return. Remember, the idea of a Mastermind group is this: two minds are usually better than one, and often when two minds come together the synergy creates a 'third' mind – one from which both parties can benefit in terms of new ideas and mental energy. When we design our Mastermind group well, the members can, in addition, help each other apply at least three of the five core elements of the MadibaMindset:

- Choose to look for the good in all situations and in all people before acting or reacting.
- Apply self-criticism before criticising as a means of empowerment.
- Learn continuously through the habitual use of each-one-teach-one.

Now consider the above discussion on strategy and structure in terms of the Robben Island example. Before Mandela and his comrades were incarcerated on Robben Island, there was already a formal and shared value statement in place, namely the Freedom Charter. This value statement was rooted in collective beliefs and commitments, which were worth striving for and staying committed to. These beliefs in what the collective body stood for – their values – made it possible to set up and refine the necessary structures, organisation and discipline within the prison context on Robben Island. I believe that much of the energy for the prisoners on the Island was generated from and maintained by these values, structures and organisational habits. The effort was further sustained and fortified by adherence to self-discipline, routine, and resolute conviction to the values of the Freedom Charter.

Perhaps you have productive values, habits, strategies and self-disciplined structures as part of your character and make-up and the way you function; or your work environment may supply them. If your work environment does not supply these, then the work environment may be dysfunctional. But we are sometimes quick to label the workplace as dysfunctional when these things are not provided, yet we as individuals often try to function without our own structure, organisation and discipline. It is clear from his autobiography, as well as from the stories told by his compatriots, that Nelson Mandela personified, in a charming manner, an abundance of resourceful values, strategies, self-disciplined habits, structure and organisation. His leadership and the example he set on the island ensured that what was lacking and was necessary was created for those of his fellow prisoners who did not already have these characteristics 'wired in'.

Summary

This chapter is about understanding the context **necessary so that we can make things happen**. Appropriate strategies and structures can be developed based on constructive habits and positive values. In the context of habits, I have already referred to Warren Buffet. In the book *Even Buffet is Not Perfect*, Vahan Janjigian writes that Buffet 'is constantly changing and refining his strategies ... no investor can expect to become tremendously successful by simply repeating the same formulaic steps over and over again ... [they] must be willing to mould their styles and strategies as conditions warrant.' Likewise, we as individuals need to be willing to do the same whilst at the same time remaining true to our values. The problem for many of us is that our habits become our structure – the way we automatically behave and react, irrespective of the context, and often counter to what the situation demands. We still apply energy but it is not effectively focused and we do not achieve the desired result. Remember that we invest our lives in our habits! How much do you want to mould your habits to be **strategically flexible** like Mandela and Buffet?

Once we recognise an inflection point, we face a challenge that starts within a self-created context, and the ensuing struggle may contain:

- Something we want or do not want.
- If it is a not, we can turn it into a positive and record a date to start action.
- Aforesaid action can stimulate a strategy for actualisation.
- A structure can then be developed to operate within.
- Positive habits can energise the strategy and, based on values, develop conviction – energy flows where attention goes.
- Use flexibility and rigorous self-honesty to monitor achievement against the desired outcome.

- There should be adaptability and willingness to be flexible and change strategy and tactics, even structure, should achievement not meet goals.

My research convinces me that the Robben Island graduates, and many others, did all of the above and more, sometimes consciously and many times instinctively. They did not record in detail how they did it so I have put together my own model, which I believe to be an implementable method, to reconcile the techniques described in this book with the tools necessary to apply them all to life and business. In the next chapter I offer a strategy for the development of your own freedom charter.

How the MadibaMindset was applied to writing this chapter (and this book)

More than 10 years ago I recognised that the MadibaMindset was indigenous South African history, sometimes anchored on the Robben Island World Heritage Site, which could be modelled productively and for the benefit of all who wish to learn from it. I presented some MadibaMindset workshops in Cape Town – initially assisted by Derrick Grootboom, and later by Indres Naidoo. Over time I became frustrated and discouraged (moving away from motivation) because it seemed that these learnings were being ignored and that there was no codified modelling text available as an instruction manual. This was mostly because I took so long to ask myself, what can I do about it regardless?

Having asked myself this question I approached James McIntosh to help. My objective was to bring strategy, structure, discipline and a Mastermind effect to the development. James and I workshopped the idea and specified an outcome for the project. We used the procedure described in Chapter 4 and initiated a move towards motivation. Since then this fairly democratic process has been replaced with a more mutually dictatorial process to make things happen. The mutually dictatorial process can best be described as each-one-pushes-one – when lagging in effort and output. Later Geraldene Corder joined the team to assist with completion, compilation and presentation.

The general suggestions that I put to James about writing Chapter 3 included that I make a few important points within what seems a somewhat light discussion. James quickly realised how important the content of Chapter 3 could be and pushed me until I did not feel the same need to lighten up on this important subject. Quite rightly, this chapter became a serious response to my initial thoughts, which included the following:

- Originally the South African anti-apartheid movement, which was later represented by the ANC and its strategies for success, some of which are modelled here, could only express its vision in terms of anti-apartheid/anti-government statements. Professor ZK Matthews then declared that this was not good enough and suggested that a positive statement describing the vision is what was needed. This suggestion was embraced by the Congress of the People and they formulated the Freedom Charter. The Freedom Charter document is free of negations – it contains only positive statements using win-win terminology.
- Energy flows where attention goes. Because the Congress of the People, and the Freedom Charter which flowed from it, attracted widespread attention, a huge amount of energy was put into its actualisation.
- The Freedom Charter became a source of universal beliefs and values, conviction and even a source of discipline for the community and it spread worldwide.
- This, in turn, led to appropriate structures and organisations being created from scratch and out of nothing.

When considering how this miracle happened, remember that Alexander Hamilton, one of the Founding Fathers of the United States of America, once said that **'those who stand for nothing fall for anything'**. Do you know what you stand for? All the preceding chapters have been aimed at getting you to understand and admit the following:

You will only be free to be yourself, to live with conviction, when what you stand for matters more to you than what other people might think.

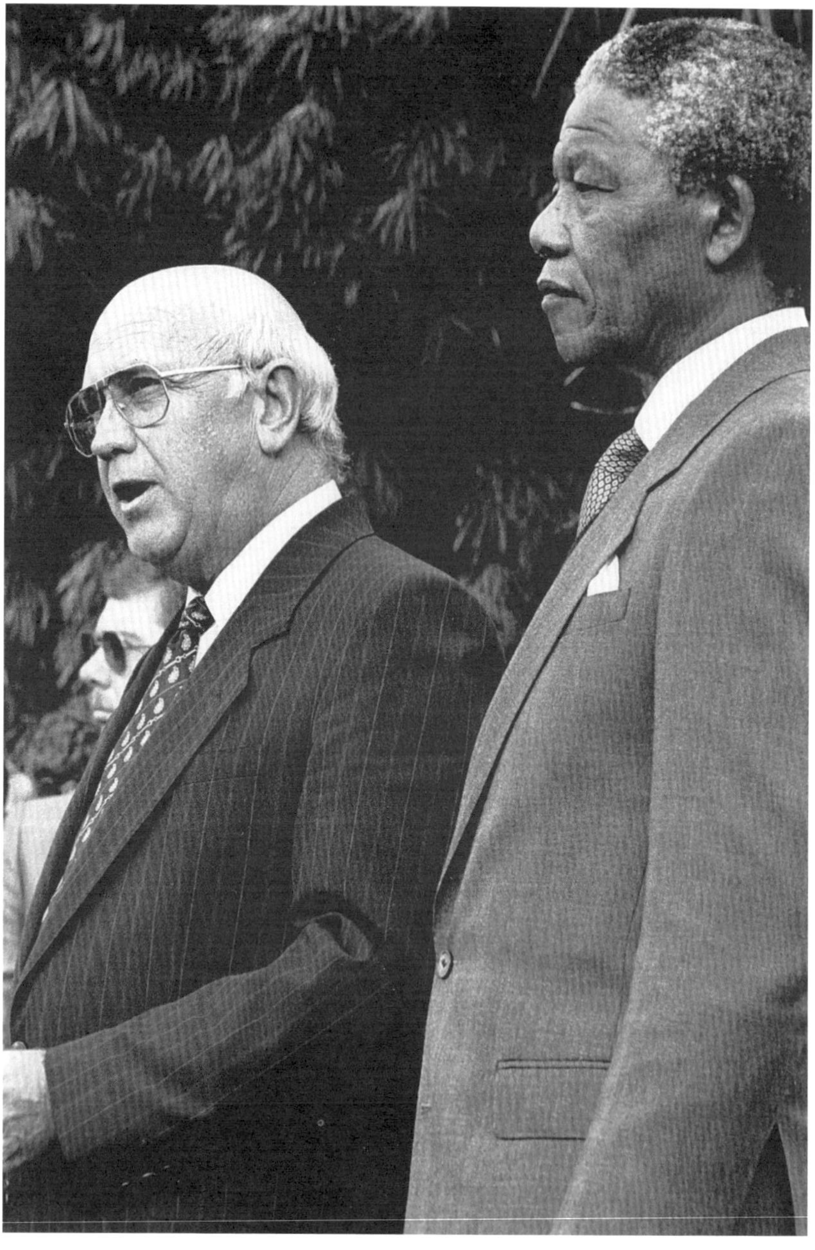

4

Write your own freedom charter

I was far more certain in those days of what I was against than what I was for.
Nelson Mandela
Long Walk to Freedom (p. 104)

PREVIOUS CHAPTERS RECORD MANY things I found useful about how the Freedom Charter was put together and how it was practised during the South African political struggle. When I faced the question of how we can do this ourselves I found no record of specific steps to do so. Over time I developed my own procedure. I have recorded this sequentially below, and present it as a model so that we can draw up our own freedom charter more easily. The following recipe developed over time, starting with an impromptu presentation I did, entitled 'Programmed Dreaming', to the New York Training Institute for NLP. NeuroLinguistic Programming is a model of how we, rather than the circumstances we face, create our own experience of life. Programmed Dreaming was developed further when designing a MadibaMindset programme for The Pavilion Conference Centre in Cape Town. No doubt a lot of the process was influenced by copious reading and research, always mindful of the filter described in the first paragraph of Chapter 2. Programmed Dreaming came to me spontaneously, and the ABCDEF steps set out later in this chapter were definitely stimulated by prior study of Genie Laborde's book *Influencing with Integrity*, which I highly recommend. I doubt Mandela ever read Laborde's book but he definitely developed his own methods of carrying out the title. He is as masterful as one can possibly be in the field of influencing with integrity!

The purpose of this chapter is to write your own freedom charter. The body of the chapter discusses how **you can**. The exercises at the end are to make it easier for you to draw up your own charter. We tend to think about a lot of things we want and nothing happens because the universe acknowledges action not thought. When we use the steps that follow we can start a process that turns our thoughts into actions, and the results we want. The first step is summarised by the letters DGOD (the sequence of the last three letters are purely coincidental, to be interpreted as you wish). This step is a helpful process to format our minds to be ready for action.

Dreams: We process thoughts about what we would like to do, to have, or not. Think about these thoughts that can just swirl around in your head and lead to nothing; ask yourself what is the most important and make a note of it. For a long time before the 1955 Congress of the People, black South Africans thought about a society without apartheid.

Goals: Tony Robbins says that 'a goal is a dream with a deadline'. I add to this, at this stage, the 'deadline' is the date when you start to do this procedure so you can write the date down now. Undoubtedly the organisers of the Congress of the People wrote down the date on which this event was to be held. Have you written down your start date?

Outcome: NLP suggests that most goals are not well formed. Well-formedness increases the likelihood of actualisation by turning goals into outcomes. The ABCDEF procedure that follows describes how you can do this. As previously suggested, the question 'What can I do about this regardless of what anyone else does?' was one of the ways used in the struggle to achieve well-formed goals. You can also write down when you want to start ABCDEF now.

Done: Constantly, and with flexibility, monitor your results versus your goal. If the results are not congruent it may well be time to change the action plan. This is addressed in more detail under step F below and was definitely done during the struggle. Often this process involves setting another date, acknowledging that achievement is a continuous and flexible process, and embraces constant and never-ending refinements, with a sequence of dates to start and finish. Remember, we seek progress rather than perfection.

As soon as you follow the first three steps outlined above you will write down a goal. This is the first step of achievement and includes a date when you start to reform the goal into an outcome. This is what the Congress of the People did when they created a vision and moved from their anti-apartheid goal to the Freedom Charter. To define your outcome, follow the ABCDEF process as follows and you will form your goal well.

Aim for the positive: If your goal includes negatives, as did the anti-apartheid dream, make it a positive by repeatedly asking, 'So what do I actually want?' Ask what it is that you actually want until you achieve a positive statement. Some of us get so stuck in negatives that we end up with statements like, I don't want to not be able to vote. If this happens to you, then realise that what you actually mean is that you do want to vote! In that case, specify your goal as something you want to happen – a positive statement. The importance of this is highlighted by the positive energy unleashed after Professor ZK Matthews suggested that being **against** apartheid was not enough and that the **anti**-apartheid movement had to decide what it was **for**.

Be in control: Ensure that the statement does not depend upon someone else doing something. We need to be in charge of activating the process. There were strategic changes during the struggle that were purposefully made to ensure that, although the goal was to change the government, the struggle actions remained in the control of the ANC. Write a list of the things **you can do** – conducive to achieving your outcome – that are within your control and the scope of the resources available to you. Monitor this list so that you have a record of progress to refer to.

C (see), hear, feel: Be sensory specific in formulating your goal. Stripped of jargon, the essence of NLP is a model of how we create our own reality using our senses and physiology. The more we intensify our sensory and physical representations, the more real and compelling our thoughts can become. The goal here is to imagine what we will see, hear and feel once we actualise our outcome. Linguistically, Nelson Mandela may not be the greatest speaker, but he does have a warm presence and wonderful smile. Thus he stimulates rapport and good feelings as well as being visually pleasing and reassuring. This kind of demeanour keeps the listener's attention and reinforces all he says despite his sometimes dry but more importantly **wise words**.

Dovetail: This expresses the essential requirement for win-win results. The carpenter's dovetail joint relies on the strength of both pieces of wood as well as the craftsman's skill. The reputation of the carpenter, the quality of the product and the satisfaction of the users all depend on the workmanship and the strength of the dovetail. Mutually beneficial results are ecological and, I believe, have more chance of succeeding and lasting once manifested. The question that needs to be asked at this point is whether everyone involved can benefit from the outcome. The Freedom Charter was designed to address and dovetail the needs of all South Africans. It is specifically crafted to address the needs of all the people of South Africa.

Engage the future: This step lets you dream again. Begin to imagine the future when your goals are materialising, and experience in advance what you may see, hear or feel when it starts to happen. I know from experience that often I strive to achieve something and only when it happens do I realise that it's not really what I want. To avoid such a waste of time and energy this way of engaging the future can help confirm your intent of continuing to pursue your goal, or it can negate it. The goal is to do a mental preview of achieving our goal and decide how much we like it. Otherwise it's like making travel plans and not looking at pictures of or reading about where you are going. You get there and really don't like what you see and hear, and then you feel awful about making the trip. As the old saying goes, 'an ounce of prevention is worth a pound of cure.' Off and on Robben Island there was a debating culture that continually previewed the design and format of the strategies, the objectives and the related outcomes that were envisaged. Regular assessment and revision, where necessary, were applied and this resulted in a refinement of ideas, style and techniques, so improving progress towards completion. Another positive benefit of this process is that it keeps the dream alive and energised. This ongoing interchange and communication during the struggle entrenched and universalised the belief that 'victory is certain', and most certainly perpetuated energy and activity both inside and outside the prison.

Flexibility and feedback: As you implement your strategy for achieving your goal it is essential to constantly compare what you are achieving relative to your goals. This is where you reconnect with the Done step discussed earlier. It is also time to ask yourself whether you have done what you planned to do.

If you are achieving your goal by doing something else then, for the record and to facilitate replication, revise your strategy. If you are not executing the original strategy and not achieving your goal, then it may be necessary to be more disciplined and change the content of your efforts to your strategy. If you are implementing your strategy and not achieving your goal, **be flexible**. Refine your strategy, its structure and application, and review its context to determine whether there is an inflection point. Because 'victory is certain', there is no failure, only feedback. Nevertheless, to continue to do the same things with more intensity and expect different results to those you have repeatedly achieved is usually considered a sign of insanity. Both Nelson Mandela's actions and words are filled with flexibility in terms of achieving goals in new and more effective ways.

While I was writing the above, the radio was on and NPR (National Public Radio in the USA) was reporting on developments at the United Nations. For more than eight years, this organisation was frozen by dogma. Now new flexibility in attitudes is dovetailing the leading democracies and some majority decisions are finally being made. The downside is massive, requiring support, cooperation and commitment so that this new approach and modus operandi can become more effective and productive in achieving its purpose. Nevertheless the rogue states are progressively being put on their back feet. As the unity between those states with a higher moral purpose solidifies, so they become stronger. This also works at the level of individuals who know what they stand for.

Richard Stengel (who helped Mandela write his autobiography) wrote in an article how he learned from Mandela that 'nothing is black or white ... when I began my interviews, I would often ask Mandela questions like this one: when you decided to suspend the armed struggle, was it because you realised you did not have the strength to overthrow the government or because you could win over international opinion by choosing nonviolence? He would then give me a curious glance and say, why not both?' Stengel writes that he did then learn to start asking smarter questions but the message was clear – life is never either/or: 'Mandela's calculus was always, what is the end that I seek, and what is the most practical way to get there?' (The article *Mandela: His 8 Lessons of Leadership* appeared on Time.com in July 2008.)

The foregoing procedures can be learned, modelled and replicated. My experience convinces me that they need to be applied with objective maturity, which happens when we start to break out of our own mental prisons and change our habits. Mandela reluctantly admitted to Richard Stengel that after 27 years in prison, 'I came out mature.' In this context, one of the challenges is to be able to consciously choose between fight, flight or negotiate. This, amongst other things, requires sufficient **humility** to realise that, however strong you are, you seldom win a fight in the long-term!

Write your own freedom charter

You now have enough information to **develop and draw up your own freedom charter**. The following exercises are designed to prompt your thinking and to guide you through the process. Please do these exercises with passion and approach them knowing that **conviction creates energy**.

Write your own freedom charter

Think out of the box

- Sit quietly for a moment ... and begin to becalm your thoughts.

- Imagine you are locked up in a cell slightly wider than your body length.

- Look up and start to visualise what you can see out of the window, which is about one foot square in size.

- What can you see outside and beyond the metal bars?

- How far and how clearly do you manage to see beyond the bars?

- Using your imagination, start entering into the MadibaMindset, and so commence your transformation into a more effective and productive existence.

- Write down what you saw beyond the bars.

Programmed Dreaming

- **Dream** – think about what you would like and write your thoughts down.

- **Goal** – write down the date when you will start the ABCDEF steps towards your goal.

- **Outcome** – write down some steps you can take, regardless of what anyone else does, to help you achieve your goal.

- **Done** – you can feel very good when you have! How do you feel about what you have done so far?

Form it well

- **Aim for the positive** – check the goal you wrote down and be sure it is positive. If not, ask yourself 'What do I really want?' and repeat until the goal is stated positively.

- Write it in positive terms before you go to the next step.

- **Be in control** – use O from the previous procedure to write a list of things you can do that are conducive to achieving your goal.

- Do the things on the list and check them off when done.

- **C (see), hear and feel** what the results of your goal will be like. Imagine what it would be like to achieve your goal. Use your imagination and be sure you get a response in all three senses. Use the 'Think out of the box' exercise to get you going if you want. Write down what these three sensory messages are.

- **Dovetail** – are these results mutually beneficial? If not, how can you refine them or revise them to make them so? If you need to, repeat the ABC exercise. Proceed once you have dovetailed.

- **Engage the future** – once again, using all of your senses, imagine what it will be like when you arrive at your goal. If it's good, proceed. If not, start again from D – the first step of the first sequence right at the beginning of the Programmed Dreaming exercise.

- **Flexibility and feed back** – ask yourself the questions in the following exercise and write down all the answers.

Be flexible
Ask yourself the following questions and write down the answers.

- Have I done what I planned to do?

- Am I achieving the results I wanted? If you answered yes twice, this exercise is now complete.

- If I am getting what I want and doing what I did not plan, what am I doing?

- If you are not getting what you want and not doing what you planned, do the plan.

- If you are doing the plan and not getting what you want, review the context to be sure it has not changed.

- Then **start again and redo the plan**. This requires a new beginning. Write down the first step to trigger the process.

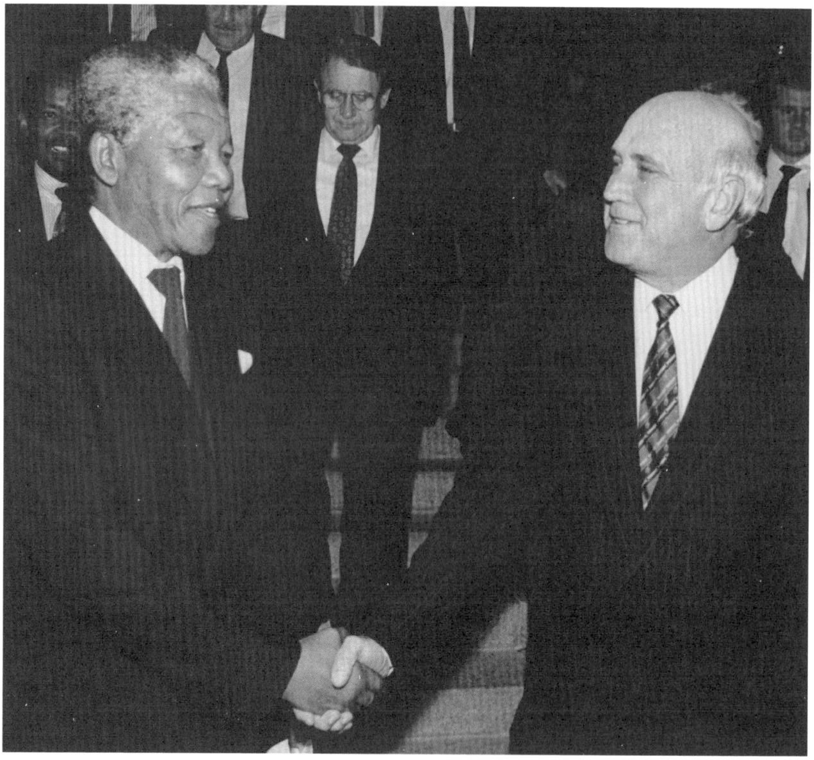

5

What you can do

If you are in harmony with yourself, you may meet a lion without fear, because he respects anyone with self-confidence.
NELSON MANDELA
In the Words of Nelson Mandela (p. 137)

THIS CHAPTER DOES NOT introduce anything new. It is more about doing and wiring in some of the previous material. I have read an enormous amount of useful material. Did I **do the suggested writing and procedures**? When I did not, I seldom fully enabled myself to experience the benefits of the reading. However, all is not lost because our unconscious minds remember. Generally we are simultaneously aware of up to seven, plus or minus two, things going on at any one time. We are also doing, or not doing, lots of other things – like breathing, balancing and other background activities – of which we are not consciously aware. These automatic activities are controlled by our unconscious minds. If we ignore something that is important to us our unconscious mind tends to remember, to remind us, and so tries to look after our best interests. Often we do not immediately recognise these unconscious good intentions. Most problem drinkers, when exposed to the Alcoholics Anonymous (AA) programme, do not immediately start the suggested constructive procrastination. However, the unconscious mind – part of which is running the addiction – also remembers that the programme is available and this memory often triggers the procrastination. Think about what internal fights and flights carry on in these circumstances, and how positive the results of negotiation can be.

In a similar vein, there are a few things that could inhibit you from doing what is required in Chapters 3 and 4. These are beliefs, habits, values, negotiating and selling. To do what is suggested by these chapters is something you can already start now. I believe that we can **do the MadibaMindset** and, supported by this belief – the stronger the better – we can get going, learn to do what we don't already know how to do, do what we already can, and so be able to do it all! In the context of the MadibaMindset, beliefs are all those things that presently we hold to be true about it. Richard Stengel wrote of Mandela when he was sentenced that 'the man who walked onto Robben Island in 1964 was emotional, headstrong, and easily stung'. These characteristics gave Mandela the beliefs and behaviours necessary to continue the struggle and to know that 'victory is certain'. However, as the struggle progressed he had to learn many new skills, strategies and behavioural changes, over all the years it took. The beliefs, and other mindsets, which Mandela and his fellows had about the struggle are massively empowering, and can help us overcome resource-based and other limiting factors. The prisoners faced huge obstacles and rose above them.

We may also have beliefs that tell us that we cannot do what is necessary. These are limiting beliefs; they hold us back, and stop us from getting started. These are our mental prisons. At the conscious level, negative beliefs, which are sometimes true concerning a lack of skills needed to succeed, can be useful whilst they temporarily remain true. We can use these temporary truths as motivation to learn the necessary skills. At the unconscious level we may have deep-seated limiting beliefs, which perhaps originated because we are trying to live somebody else's dreams or programming. Sometimes these beliefs stop us from doing what we can and want to. The good news is we can be headstrong enough, like Mandela, to **overcome these limiting beliefs**. Psychologists spend a lot of time working out why we have these beliefs but finding the reason why often does not help. We can change the belief from I can't to **I can**. Then the why becomes irrelevant as the limiting belief has disappeared. This, I believe, is the most practical and easiest way to escape limiting beliefs. The subject or field of beliefs is extremely broad so, at the risk of over simplification, I suggest you ask yourself the following questions concerning any limiting beliefs you may have. Do this first in respect

What you can do

of your own freedom charter – whether it is about preparation or implementation, or both. You will find an exercise sheet that you can copy and work on at the end of this chapter. Exercise sheets are previewed in the chapter to make it easier to use them prolifically.

Uncovering your limiting beliefs

Write down the context in which you consider the following questions. In other words, write down what the context is in the heading phrase. It could be your work, a specific project, a skill you want to master, a relationship issue or something else.

- Sit quietly for a moment after you calm your thoughts.
- Read and consider the following questions carefully and deeply:
  - What prevents me from doing this? (Clarify and name 'this'.)
  - What will happen when I can do this? (Clarify and name 'this'.)
  - How can I pretend I can do this before I start doing it?
  - How do I feel about being able to do it and doing it?
  - How far am I towards changing this belief to 'I can'?
  - How have I changed this belief to 'I can'?
- Now review your written answers to the above questions.

The above questions start a process towards overcoming limiting beliefs. However, the energy driving the process springs from our values. Our values are those things we believe to be important (if you are still unsure or unclear about this, refer to the section on values in Chapter 3). The more important something is to us, the more upset we are if it does not happen and the more effort we are prepared to exert to make it happen. Once it starts to happen we can be massively pleased and happy. We have both 'towards' and 'away from' values; previously we referred to these as things we want, and things we don't want. In the struggle for freedom, access to education and opportunities – as well as respect and dignity – were extremely important values. The apartheid policy denied access to these human rights so that anti-apartheid became a massive 'away' – from community value. The Freedom Charter changed it to a seductively appealing 'towards' value. When you change a belief and learn new skills to pursue your own freedom charter it is important to make sure that your values give you conviction. Remember that when Mandela was sentenced on treason charges he said to the world from the dock, when faced with the ultimate sentence, that he had committed his life to the struggle and, if necessary, was prepared to die for it.

The values empowering the MadibaMindset are of the highest possible order. To check the importance of the values behind your outcome as expressed in your own freedom charter, ask yourself – again aided by the exercise sheet at the end of this chapter – the following questions:

Checking the importance of your values against your outcomes

- Sit quietly for a moment after you calm your thoughts.
- Answer the following questions carefully and in writing:
    - What is most important to me about this outcome? (Clarify and name the 'outcome'.)
    - How much more important is this outcome than a belief that it can't happen?
    - Does this outcome support the other things I have and don't have that are important?
    - How vital is it that I can start to do it?
    - How does 'I can do this outcome' support my important values?
- Now review your written answers to each of the above questions.

The exercise above deals with your outcomes as recorded in your freedom charter. Remember that this is different to the goal you also recorded in the DGOD recipe. For this reason there is also an exercise sheet relevant to your goals at the end of the chapter. You can **use it in the same way.**

These value energisers are essential, so remember you may want to use each-one-teach-one to get them in order if necessary. Yes, you can find somebody skilled in values work and do a trade exchange so that you let go completely of any limiting beliefs. Limiting beliefs are mental prisons and, like a Robben Island graduate, you can set yourself free from their shackles. Do you understand that in the above process you were negotiating with yourself? Whether we are children or adults we are always negotiating, although we often avoid negotiation and respond with fight or flight. Regardless, and whether we realise it or not, some are better negotiators than others although we all negotiate.

What you can do

You can now embrace the concept that in the question-and-answer session above you were negotiating with yourself and not fighting or running away. Perhaps you will, if you did not before, **believe now that you can and do negotiate**. The choice is not whether you do it but rather how well you do. In the next chapter we will be following some of FW de Klerk's negotiation models. This introduces some useful principles and skills that include:

- Developing and maintaining rapport.
- Finding a level of agreement with almost everyone.
- Choosing purposefully when to be abstract and when to be more specific.
- Negotiating and selling, which have a lot in common.
- Dovetailing to be successful according to the MadibaMindset principles.

Many of us have mental blocks and limiting beliefs about selling. How often do we hear, sometimes from our own inner voice, that I can't sell or I never want to have to sell anything? Usually this attitude is stimulated by a bad experience with a salesperson who, wanting to make a quick buck, did not have the buyer's interests at heart. Abusive salespeople usually have quick money as a high or highest value and give the word 'sell' a bad reputation. Regardless, the *Oxford English Dictionary* defines 'sell' as 'to inspire someone to possess'. Remember that the word 'possess' means far more than 'buy' because the resultant experience usually lasts for a much longer time. We can think of ideas and things we possess and realise that we have long-term constructive relationships as a result of the inspirations that led us to possess them. Remember also that the *Oxford English Dictionary* suggests that inspiration is a 'suggestion coming from an influential person'.

You may realise that knowing what is important to the other person and dovetailing are essential if you want to inspire, even yourself. As you fully consider all of the foregoing, you may remember that FW de Klerk influenced his constituency to transfer power to the much-feared party of the masses. He could do this because he was convinced that it was in their country's long-term best interests. He opened up the potential benefits of democracy supported by a liberal constitution that entrenches the rule of law. Almost simultaneously, Mandela influenced his people to give up the armed struggle and negotiate with the enemy. After Mandela won the subsequent election he inspired the white minority, previously the ruling class, to respect his rule and to admire him. He could do this because he truly believed that, according to the Freedom Charter, all the people should benefit from the new democracy.

De Klerk and Mandela, both lawyers by training, learned to become master salespeople, negotiate the biggest sales ever in the world, and to earn a Nobel Peace Prize for doing so! Can you imagine anything more honourable than selling when you consider their achievement? In the next chapter we will suggest a few useful principles and strategies for both negotiating and selling. However, before moving on to Chapter 6, we suggest that you now do those exercises in this chapter you have not already done. Exercise sheets follow.

What you can do

Uncovering your limiting beliefs concerning something important – 'X'

- Write down the context in which you will consider the following questions. In other words, write down what 'X' is in the heading of this exercise. It could be your work, a specific project, a skill you want to master, a relationship issue, etc.

- Sit quietly for a moment after you calm your thoughts.

- Read and consider the following questions carefully and deeply:
  – What prevents me from doing this? (Clarify and name 'this'.)
  – What will happen when I can do this? (Clarify and name 'this'.)
  – How can I imagine I can do this before I start doing it?
  – How do I feel about being able to do it and doing it?
  – How far am I towards changing this belief to 'I can'?
  – How have I changed this belief to 'I can'?

- Now review your written answers to each of the above questions.

Checking the importance of your values against your outcomes

- Sit quietly for a moment after you calm your thoughts.

- Answer the following questions carefully and in writing:
  - What is most important to me about this outcome? (Clarify and name 'outcome'.)
  - What will I see, hear and feel when this outcome occurs?
  - How much more important is this outcome than a belief that it can't happen?
  - Does this outcome support the other things I have and don't have that are important?
  - How valuable is it that I can start to do it?
  - How does 'I can do this outcome' support my important values?

- Now review your written answers to each of the above questions.

Checking the importance of your values against your goals

- Sit quietly for a moment after you calm your thoughts.

- Answer the following questions carefully and in writing:
  - What is most important to me about this goal? (Clarify and name your 'goal'.)
  - What will I see, hear and feel when this goal is realised?
  - How much more important is this goal than a belief that it can't happen?
  - Does this goal support the other things I have and don't have that are important?
  - How valuable is it that I can start to do it?
  - How does 'I can do this goal' support my important values?

- Now review your written answers to each of the above questions.

Understanding the importance of selling

- Sit quietly for a moment after you calm your thoughts.

- Read the dictionary definitions in the chapter for 'sell' and 'inspire', write them down, and remember them after you fully consider them.

- List some of your regular activities, which you now realise are selling. How could all involved benefit when you learn to sell better?

- List the sales activities necessary from your previously recorded freedom charter.

- Record how important it is for all that you do a great selling job.

- Record why the choice is not whether you sell, but whether you **do it well** and **dovetail** every time you negotiate a sale!

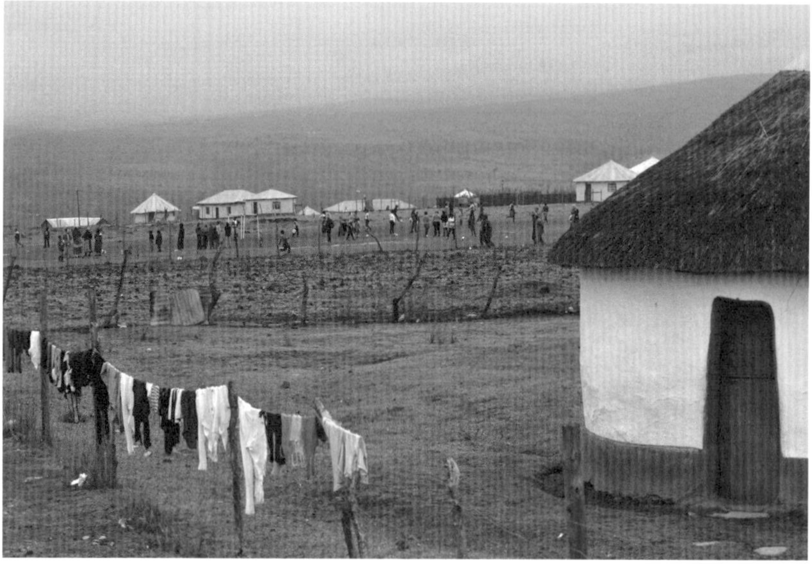

6

How you can do it

When I focus beyond the self ... I have access to a much grander form of awareness.
SIDNEY POITIER
The Measure of a Man (p. 204)

MANY TIMES IN PREVIOUS chapters I encouraged focused uninterrupted attention. Yet we live in a world filled with millions of distractions. These are often experienced in the form of pictures, words, maybe a nagging voice in your head – and feelings. Sometimes the distractions are internally generated and sometimes they are externally generated. Regardless of the source, a restless state of mind may follow. To overcome a stressful feeling, Nelson Mandela used humour, which was extremely effective for him. This is how he explains it in *Mandela – The Authorised Portrait*: 'Even when you are discussing a serious matter relaxation is very important because it encourages your thinking, so I like to make jokes even when examining serious situations. Because when people are relaxed they can think properly.' (p. 345).

The following steps, meditative in nature, describe how you can stimulate peace of mind regardless of how good you are at making jokes:

Stimulate peace of mind
(To make a working copy, see the end of this chapter.)

- Find a comfortable, relatively upright chair and sit up straight,

rest your feet flat on the ground, and gently touch your hands on your thighs.
- Look straight ahead and slightly up; find something relatively small, and fix your eyes on it. Look for some detail in that something and focus your attention on this for a few seconds. Then allow your vision to spread out panoramically, as if you are looking through a wide-angle lens, so that you see what is ahead more expansively as you move from focused to panoramic vision.
- You may notice spontaneous noises at times and when you do, say to yourself: I can let these sounds be soothing and relaxing before they float away.
- As you retain your broader panoramic view, become aware of your breathing. Breathe in through your nose and then exhale through your mouth. Extend your exhale so that you breathe out for twice as long as you inhale through your nose. Repeat this quite a few times, while you stay in panoramic vision. Practise this breathing sequence, always breathing in through the nose and out of the mouth for twice as long, while thinking of the big picture – a panoramic view. Remember, all sounds are soothing and relaxing while you do this, before they fade away naturally.
- As you continue to breathe like this allow yourself to become aware of the space above you and behind, and outside of the room; maybe you can recall something in this space and visualise it. If your awareness is still inside the room let it float outside and become aware of all that is outside as you continue to breathe in through your nose and out through your mouth for twice as long. Keep your awareness outside while you breathe easily and let all sounds be soothing and relaxing so that you feel comfortable and peaceful. That's right, you can feel peace of mind all over, and as you sit comfortably you can start from the beginning and **learn to do this exercise naturally and easily whenever you want to do it.**

In *The Measure of a Man,* quoted at the start of this chapter, Sidney Poitier wrote that: 'Los Angeles is part of a state, and that this state is part of the country, and that this country is part of a hemisphere, and that this hemisphere is part of a globe, and that this globe is one of nine or eleven (depending on your point of view) planets that move around the sun ...' After you consider this quote you can imagine

How you can do it

the Robben Island prisoner who saw the stars as he stared through the bars of his cell, and how it enabled him to be calm, positive and orientated to a new future.

Use the foregoing exercise repeatedly whenever you feel the need, and always before you do the exercises in this book, and both before and after you read. Your goal is that it becomes a habit. Then you can do it in mini form, quickly and easily, when you feel the need to relax and recollect yourself. You may even become better at it, as you learn and understand the model of how the mind receives and processes information that follows this short anecdote.

At the time of the 'thinking properly' conversation at Mandela's home in 2005 (quoted above) there was much discussion about a previously indecipherable note in Mandela's handwriting. It was written at the end of the Treason Trial and contained notes for a speech that he never got the opportunity to make. The court procedure at the time was that once the judge had decided on the death penalty he would, prior to announcing it, ask the accused, 'Have you any reason why the death sentence should not be passed?' The night before sentencing Mandela set about preparing for this possibility of the next morning. The notes he made then were discussed in 2005 and it was agreed that the gist of the speech he intended to make was:

'What I said in the dock I am prepared to stand by ... [the 'I am prepared to die' speech quoted before, and made some seven weeks before sentencing], ... this thing is growing, these people who have shed blood, will continue, the army is growing, I want everyone to know that I am not backing off. I stand by everything I said and if I must die I will meet my fate like a man .... So your look was straight, only on the future, and it was not about you, it was entirely about the struggle.' The foregoing was articulated by Mac Maharaj and Mandela twice replied, 'I remember that very well and ... that's true!'

Mac Maharaj said later during the same conversation, as recorded in *Mandela – The Authorised Portrait*, 'This was one of the most moving speeches in Africa. A speech you did not get a chance to make because you were not sentenced to death!' (p. 345)

How the mind receives and processes information

4. Conscious mind (outputs)

Our behaviours are the result of 1, 2 and 3, including physiology. Everything that happens in our life is affected by the choices we make and is communicated via our senses and internal feelings.

1. Conscious mind (inputs)

Ears pick up sounds.
Eyes pick up sights.
Nose picks up smells.
Skin picks up feelings (senses).

Millions of inputs!

3. Unconscious processing

What we choose not to pay attention to is processed unconsciously. Our unconscious mind decides how to process that information. However, what we believe and value greatly influences how it's done.
This in turn affects our conscious processing of information.

2. Conscious or unconscious (processing)

We decide which of the above to pay attention to and how we pay attention. We delete some inputs; we distort some by reference to beliefs, values, habits, experience, etc; and we generalise.

There are over one million choices available at any moment.
At any moment, we can pay attention to seven, plus or minus two.
What we pay attention to is our conscious awareness; everything else is unconscious processing.

- Do we pay attention to what is important?
- Our values determine what is important to us.

In the context of this chapter we can be convinced that Mandela knew what was important to him, he was steadfast and, both consciously and unconsciously, he showed his total conviction. He may have had a chance to backtrack before and on D-Day, and try to save his skin, but he was not prepared to take it. He knew what was important and he paid complete and focused attention to it. Remember Milton Erickson, the American psychiatrist specialising in medical hypnosis and family therapy, who is reputed to have said that 'you can have whatever you want provided you pay … attention to what is important, and if you don't … you will pay with pain'. Mandela was prepared to pay the ultimate price for his ideals and goals and it must have been an extremely painful process. Nevertheless, for him it would have been more painful to capitulate than to pay the ultimate price! For us the question is: How do we 'normal people' specify what is important to ourselves? I learned the following values elicitation procedure from NLP and it works as follows:

Values elicitation description
(An exercise sheet is at the end of this chapter.)
- Decide the context (e.g. your work) for which you want to elicit your values. Write it down.
- Ask yourself, in the context of .... (e.g. my work), what is most important to me about ....? Make a list of what comes to you spontaneously and just write these thoughts down as they come to you (at least five and no more than 10).
- Go back and rank them in order of importance. Discard those not ranking in the top five or make the list slightly longer if more than five seem important.
- Just look at them and write a number behind them in pencil, as it comes to you instinctively. Then rewrite the list in order of importance on a blank page in pencil.
- Then start from the bottom and ask, in respect of the second-last value relative to the last, 'Is the second-last one more or less important to me than the last one?'
- Work your way up the list and ask the same question (as in the previous step) about the third-last one relative to the second-last one, and so on, until you reach your most important value – superior to the second most important one.
- Double check: start with the highest ranked value and ask yourself, 'If I have one, will it support having two?' Work down your list in the same manner and, if necessary, adjust the rankings so that higher values support those below them.
- Now ask yourself the following questions in respect of each value, and write the answers down briefly next to that value:
  – How do I know when I am ....?
  – What is the specific evidence of that?
  – What does this evidence mean to me?
  – Is there a deeper or higher purpose, useful to others as well, of this meaning?

Before or after you do this in respect of your own values you can also imagine you are Mandela facing the death sentence. Consider fully the difference between moving away from motivation and moving towards motivation:

- Was it more important to Mandela that he moved away from death;
- Or was it more important that he moved towards the liberation of his people?
- Are your values predominantly 'towards' or 'away from'?

You are unlikely to achieve much by only being against something. It is essential that you know what you are for. If your values are predominantly away from, ask yourself, in respect of each and every one of them, 'What do I really want in the context of this value?' Repeat the question as many times as is necessary to get a positive answer.

When we have positive values we can see light at the end of the tunnel. This, in the context of our work and those things we decide to do with our lives, offers a starting point to design our existence in terms of what is most important to us. Often we tend to know about, and pay too much attention to, things that can cause irritation, sadness, insecurity, doubt, anger, and so on. However, is it not more important to apply our minds to what we have natural talents for, what we find stimulating, how we can add value, and what we feel happy about doing that is also constructive? If we switch on the light in our life in this way, then the darkness will disappear and there is no longer any need to pay attention to it. This can help lead you to the work that works for you, other people, and the context of your life.

The context of Mandela's life was undoubtedly the achievement of democracy and a better life for all the people of South Africa. Essentially his commitment to the Freedom Charter was the source of his life's convictions and the struggle against oppression. In Chapter 3 we referred to the AA programme – the struggle against the oppression of addiction, and the achievement of a better life through positive procrastination. This example is a good analogy to understand the structure of oppression that usually develops because of addiction. Most addicts, prior to recovery, experience or have experienced:

1. A positive benefit from consumption.
2. Suffering from excessive consumption.
3. A desire to retain the benefit in point 1, and simultaneously move away from point 2.
4. An addiction, which is set off unconsciously, which prevents the achievement of point 3.
5. Massive frustration, fear, humiliation, rejection, and so on, as a result of point 4.

Going back many years in South Africa, the Afrikaner people (Dutch settlers) were oppressed by, and went to war with, the British to win their freedom. I recently visited a museum in Bermuda and the exhibits about Burt's Island made a deep impression on me. Burt's is the little island off Bermuda where the British imprisoned the 'Irreconcilables' – those Afrikaners/Boer prisoners of war, who protested with perpetual conviction against British rule in South Africa. A plaque quoted Isaac Joubert, a Boer POW: 'You can never imagine how cruel it is to be deprived of your liberty. A year's severe fighting cannot teach you as much as one month's imprisonment.' After the Afrikaners won their freedom they feared that the indigenous people would outnumber them and take away their hard-won liberty. Apartheid, and its religious justification, was invented by their prime minister at the time, namely HF Verwoerd. The Afrikaner nation was attracted to it because it had the positive benefits of offering to keep control of the country to themselves and, being a religious nation, it was doubly attractive because their church told them that it was God's will. Thus they became addicted to it and it led to the oppression of the people of colour. Mandela understood this even though he despised it. He was therefore better able to work with and develop relationships with his Afrikaner oppressors when he got the opportunity, starting with the prison guards, and later negotiating with government officials.

To work out the original positive purpose of destructive behaviours, whether by people or governments, it is useful to learn the following Hierarchy of Ideas. It is another model from NLP of how thoughts and their expression, within the same context, can move from being abstract and vague to being precise and specific, and vice versa. I have no doubt that Sidney Poitier understands this hierarchy, at least in terms of tangibles as opposed to ideas. This is why he articulated the Los Angeles sequence, as quoted earlier, so clearly. Although it is often said that the 'devil is in the detail', the most important information is somewhere in the abstract because it contains all the detail within it.

Hierachy of Ideas in the context of freedom

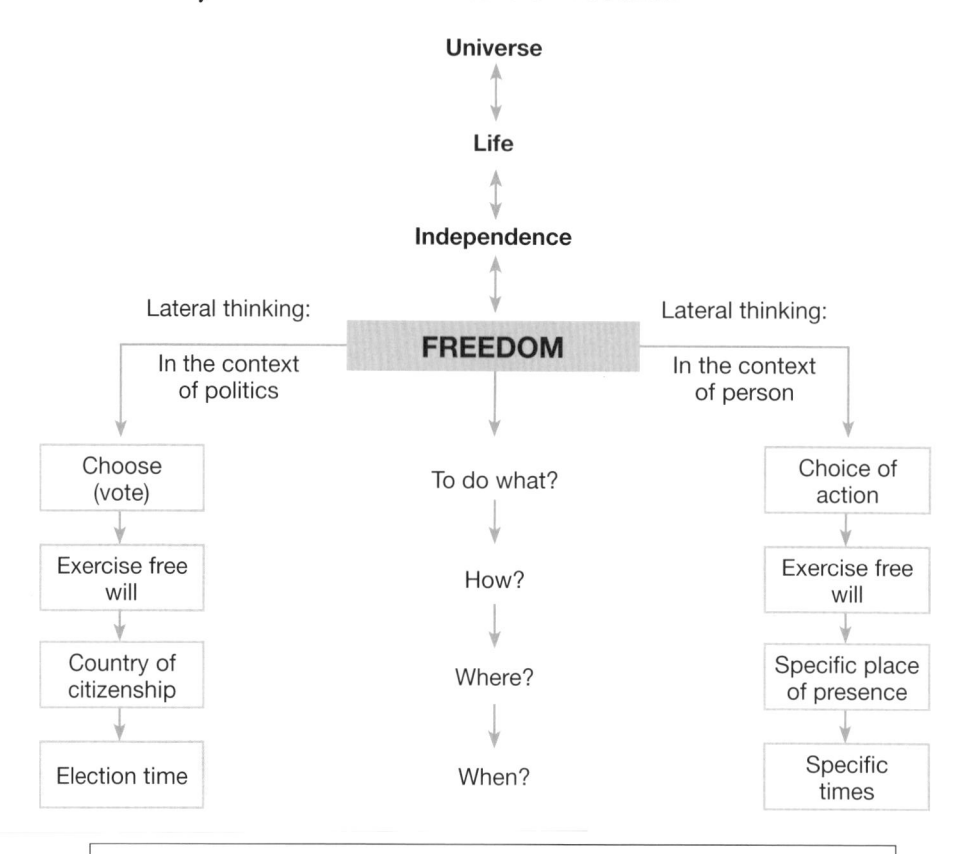

```
                        Universe
                           ↕
                          Life
                           ↕
                       Independence
                           ↕
  Lateral thinking:      FREEDOM       Lateral thinking:
  In the context           ↓           In the context
  of politics                           of person
```

In the context of politics		In the context of person
Choose (vote)	To do what?	Choice of action
↓	↓	↓
Exercise free will	How?	Exercise free will
↓	↓	↓
Country of citizenship	Where?	Specific place of presence
↓	↓	↓
Election time	When?	Specific times

> Different contexts stimulate lateral thinking.
> Each higher level contains the detail below it and the question 'What is this a part of?' can lead to it.
> Each lower level is a part of the classification above it and the question 'What is a part of this?' can lead to it.

Note: The recipe of this diagram is an essential tool that you can use when deciding what is important to do; and when negotiating, thinking laterally, and communicating, among other things.

In addition, the Hierarchy of Ideas is a description of freedom in a 'moving towards' positive context. This presupposes that there is no oppression like apartheid or an addiction, from which a society 'or individual' first has to free itself before it can exercise its full spectrum of choices. The process of moving between different logical levels is often called chunking – that is, **chunking up** from precise to abstract, and **chunking down** from abstract to precise. In the following exercise I suggest you practise chunking as follows:

Practise chunking up and down
(To make a working copy, see the end of this chapter.)
It is usually easier to start with concrete nouns although sometimes more interesting to start with abstract nouns. Usually you will end up with both in the hierarchy, especially if you start at the concrete level.

- Write a word in the middle of a blank page. (I have suggested 'Robben Island' on the exercise page.)
- You can chunk up by asking, 'What is it a part of?' and/or questions like:
  – What is important about it?
  – For what purpose?
  – What is an example of it?
  – What is important to me about it?
- You can chunk down by asking:
  – What is a part of this?
  – How?
  – What?
  – When?
  – What is an example of this?

You will find at first that it is easier to practise with concrete nouns or things you can touch, such as cars, houses and plants. Abstract nouns refer to things – like ideas, qualities, emotions or ideals – that cannot be physically interacted with. Verbs that have been turned into abstract nouns are called nominalisations. Like the first example on page 86 of 'freedom', abstract nouns are usually more complicated although some of the skills we discussed earlier that require chunking, or can be greatly enhanced by chunking, include:

- Choose to **look for the good in all situations and/or people before acting or reacting.** As soon as you perceive any negative internal perceptions, say to yourself, **'But it's much more than that'.** The purpose of this statement is to open your mind to more possibilities before probing for specifics. Follow this by asking yourself some of the chunking up questions listed earlier or simply ask: **'And what's good about it?'**
- **In the event of disagreement**, chunk up until you find something you agree about even if it is that you have differences of opinion and want to understand both perspectives. FW de Klerk suggested that, as a last resort, 'agree on your points of departure', and make a list of them. The latter is a process of **chunking down** to the detail. By the time you finish this process you have agreed twice with your adversary, and have opened up the possibility that, despite serious differences, **you are capable of agreeing**.

The above are ways of starting to develop rapport. As Mandela said, 'solutions emerge when those who have been divided reach out to find the common ground.' Strategies to start this process comprise matching the other person in the following ways:

- Communicate initially at the same logical level before chunking up or down.
- Breathe at a similar pace.
- Speak at a similar speed.
- Adopt a harmonious posture.
- Use humour, carefully and without trivialising the issues, as recommended by Mandela.
- Find a common interest, for example family and children, as Mandela did with the guards.

These are helpful tools to generate some rapport even before any content is addressed. Many were used on Robben Island and during the South African negotiated revolution. In terms of the five-point addiction model set out earlier, the old apartheid dogma included at least:

1. A perceived benefit in terms of freedom and religious compliance.

How you can do it

2. Suffering due to the excessive application of an extremely flawed ideology.
3. A desire to restructure the political ideology and retain the perceived benefit of one.
4. Universal oppression due to ingrained programming of the flawed ideology.
5. Rejection of apartheid and South Africa by the rest of the world.

FW de Klerk saw that the country was locked in a downward spiral because of its long addiction to apartheid. The Iron Curtain came down and the only remaining international support South Africa enjoyed, which was predicated on its anti-communist stance, dissolved. Around the same time, De Klerk was presented with a great opportunity because the Dutch Reformed Church had renounced apartheid as a sin. His people were motivated to move away from this sin but were scared to move towards one-man-one-vote, which they had learned to fear from childhood. He had to do something to loosen up the thinking and open it up to possibilities, so he chunked up! Perhaps he asked himself, whether consciously or unconsciously, 'What is one-man-one-vote an example of, and how can I achieve greater freedom for my people compliant with their religious beliefs?' He invented the following, which he stated in one of his early speeches:

- 'A new system whereby everyone should have a vote of equal value.'
- An assurance that 'checks and balances would ensure that oppression of the majority by the minority would not be replaced by oppression of the minority by the majority'. It is truly interesting that this aligns entirely with Mandela's principle of democracy, which he articulated as an early learning experience at the Great Place!

De Klerk's speeches, especially with statements like the above, opened up productive thought and debate about how these goals could be achieved. He called a referendum of his voters and he received a mandate to negotiate a new democratic dispensation within the foregoing parameters. This eventually resulted in elections after which the minority handed over control of the police, the security forces and the military to the previously disenfranchised majority. The parameters De Klerk initially spelt out were specifically vague and preceded long negotiations to find a more exact formula for democracy. This process involved much fight, flight, and chunking up and down. The language he used in his speeches enabled negotiations and created challenges such as the following:

- 'Everyone' is a huge generalisation so questions such as, 'Who specifically?' had to be asked to define a qualification to vote.
- 'Should' implies possibility and desirability. Questions such as, 'What would happen if ... ?' and 'How would it be achieved?' test the validity of these implications.
- 'Vote' is, as defined previously, a nominalisation. Its meaning and effectiveness can be clarified by questions like, 'Vote for what?' and 'How would they vote?'
- 'Equal value' deletes the standard to which value is to be compared. The question 'Equal value to what?' reinstates a standard of value.

CODESA (the Convention for a Democratic South Africa) started some time after Mandela was released and preceded the first universal election. This was a long and arduous process and is covered in many texts. Despite a host of distractions and attempts to derail them, the negotiations succeeded and are regarded as an unprecedented achievement. Whether or not you have read about these negotiations, you can review the following introductory diagram, which I prepared to illustrate some important core issues about the negotiation process:

- The start point is somewhere in the middle, with the difference of opinion represented by the gap between positions A and B.
- The goal is a meeting of the minds represented by the intersection of the two lines at the bottom.
- Negotiation is usually easier in the context of rapport. Counter-intuitively the best first step is usually to chunk up, further away from the goal. This is because rapport and agreement are initially easier in vague, rather than specific, terms except when defining points of departure.
- Specific agreements are more easily reached in the context of rapport and an atmosphere of agreement.

Chunk up to abstract generalisations
Find common ground and rapport

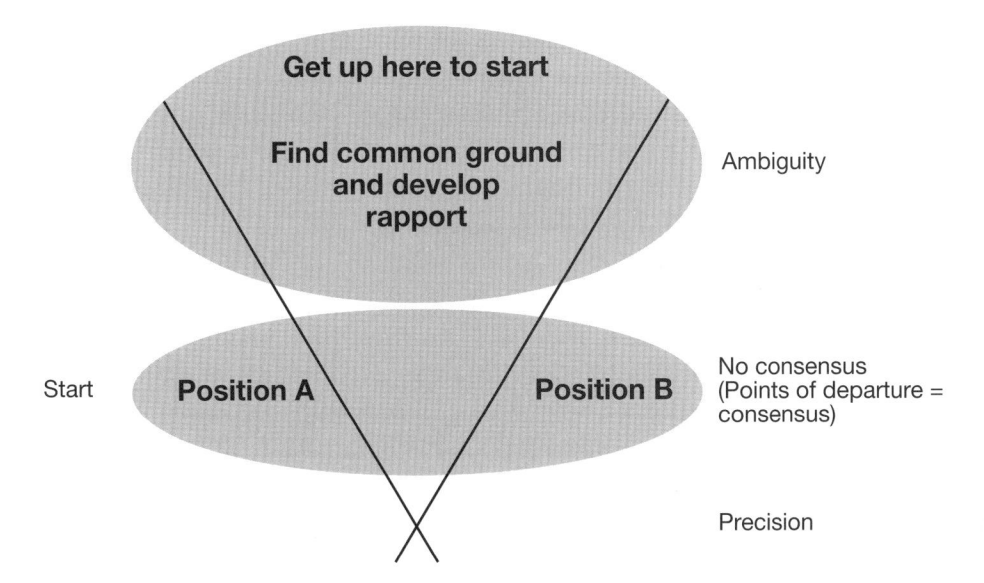

Get up here to start

Find common ground and develop rapport — Ambiguity

Start — **Position A** / **Position B** — No consensus (Points of departure = consensus)

Precision

Outcome = meeting of minds = agreement
What processes to use to achieve desired outcome?

After you fully consider the above diagram, does it make sense? If not, go back and review this chapter, starting from the Hierarchy of Ideas.

During negotiation, chunking down can, in the absence of rapport, be a nitpicking conflict generator, and can often destroy rapport. If rapport is lost it is usually advisable to restore it by chunking up again to a level where agreement already exists. Remember the core belief in democratic, rather than majority, rule which had been independently articulated by both CODESA leaders long before the event. Productive negotiation is usually a process of chunking up and down until there is a meeting of minds. At the risk of repetition, I stress some of the benefits of chunking up and down:

- If two people try to communicate from different logical levels a meeting of the minds is unlikely and irritation will probably result.

- Agreement is always available at the abstract level and this stimulates rapport, which is usually a precondition for agreement.
- The devil is in the detail and a true meeting of minds demands precision. Chunking down is the route to precise agreement.
- A negotiation process often requires a process of chunking up, then down, and then up again before being able to go further down. The above embraces the fight, flight and negotiate concept and stresses that final agreement usually happens in an atmosphere of rapport. Rapport levels tend to fluctuate.

When you embrace the relaxation, chunking, and other exercises this book describes, they will enhance your understanding and application of this Mindset. You can **experience a mindshift**. The entire negotiation of South Africa's constitutional revolution took place over many years and was a series of mindshifts. The democratic principles did not change. Consideration of the historic literature on this subject, as well as the film *Invictus*, details a process including:

- Preliminary discussions when people got to know each other and developed rapport. This started with Mandela's visit, when he was still a prisoner, to have tea with President PW Botha.
- Lengthy negotiations up to and including CODESA, which resulted in parameters for a new democratic constitution.
- Fights during the negotiation processes, which led to deadlocks and suspension (flight) of the negotiations.
- Rebuilding of rapport/negotiation, before more detailed discussion could restart.

Notice that, at some level, all of the above is going on in all of our lives regularly and repetitively. The choice is about how well to do it, and whether to get stuck in fight or flight, or not. To stress this, I suggest the following:

Inspirations
(An exercise sheet appears at the end of this chapter.)

- Watch the Clint Eastwood movie *Invictus* and/or read the book on which the Invictus movie is based, namely *Playing the Enemy*

How you can do it

- *Nelson Mandela and the Game That Made a Nation* by John Carlin (more recent editions of the book are also titled *Invictus*).
- As you enjoy watching the movie or reading the book, note specifically how your education and learning about the MadibaMindset deepens.
- Remember that the *Oxford Dictionary* defines 'sell' as to 'inspire someone to possess' and that it suggests that inspiration is a 'suggestion coming from an influential person'. With that in mind, do you understand why we make the following two points?
  - FW de Klerk made a great sale when he inspired his voters to let go of their fears and seek a new democracy.
  - At least one of Mandela's greatest sales is recorded in *Invictus*.

I believe that we can all use these skills to be more relaxed, pay attention to what is important and, in our own context and scale, to do our own *Invictus!* This movie will mean different things to all of us. In the context of this book it is all about rising above something (oppressive fear, perhaps) and getting out of our mental prison. This limiting mindset holds us back; we can identify it and then find a way to get out of its prison. The ability to do so is within you and can be released and empowered by the strategies in this book. Some of the possibilities are discussed in the following final chapter.

Stimulate peace of mind
- Find a comfortable, relatively upright chair – relax as you sit up straight, feet softly touching flat on the ground, as you quietly rest your hands on your thighs.
- Look straight ahead and slightly up; find something relatively small, and fix your eyes on it. Look for some detail in that something and focus your attention on it for a few seconds. Then allow your vision to spread out panoramically, as if you are looking through a wide-angle lens, so that you see what is ahead more expansively as you move from focused to panoramic vision.
- You may notice spontaneous noises at times and when you do, say to yourself, 'I can let these sounds be soothing and relaxing before they float away naturally.'
- As you retain your broader panoramic view, become aware of your breathing. Breathe in through your nose and then exhale through

your mouth. Extend your exhale so that you breathe out for twice as long as you inhale through your nose. Repeat this quite a few times, while you stay in panoramic vision. Practise this breathing sequence, always breathing in through the nose and out of the mouth for twice as long, while thinking of the big picture – a panoramic view. Remember, all sounds are soothing and relaxing while you do this, before they fade away naturally.

- As you continue to breathe like this allow yourself to become aware of the space above you and behind, outside of the room; maybe you can recall something in this space and visualise it. If your awareness is still inside the room, let it float outside and become aware of all that is outside as you continue to breathe in through your nose and out through your mouth for twice as long. Keep your awareness outside while you breathe easily and let all sounds be soothing and relaxing while you feel comfortable and peaceful. That's right, you can feel your peace of mind all over, and as you sit comfortably you can start from the beginning and **learn to do this exercise naturally and easily when you want to do it.**

How you can do it

Values elicitation

- Decide the context (e.g. your work) for which you want to elicit your values. Write it down.

- Ask yourself, in the context of .... (e.g. my work), what is most important to me about .... (e.g. my work)? Make a list of what comes to you spontaneously and just write these thoughts down as they come to you (not less than five and no more than 10).

- Go back and rank them in order of importance from one to five, discarding those ranking below five or make the list slightly longer if more than five seem important.

- Just look at them and write a number behind them in pencil as it comes to you instinctively. Then rewrite the list in order of importance on a blank page in pencil.

- Then start from the bottom and ask, in respect of the second-last value relative to the last, 'If I have the second-last one, is that more or less important to me than the last one?'

(*Continued overleaf*)

Values elicitation (continued)

- Work your way up the list and ask the same question as previously about the third-last one relative to the second-last one, and so on, until you finish with your most important value relative to the second most important one.

- Double check – start with the highest ranked value and ask yourself, 'If I have one, will it support having two?' Work down your list in the same manner and, if necessary, adjust the rankings so that higher values support those below them.

- Now ask yourself the following questions in respect of each value, and write the answers down briefly next to that value:
  – How do I know when I am …………………………?
  – What is the specific evidence of that?
  – What does this evidence mean to me?
  – Is there a deeper or higher purpose, meaningful to more than myself, of this?

How you can do it

Practise chunking

- Write a word in the middle of a blank page. (On the exercise on page 98, I have suggested Robben Island.)

- You can chunk up by asking, 'What is it a part of?' and/or questions such as:
  – What is important about it?
  – For what purpose?
  – What is an example of it?
  – What is important to me about it?

- You can chunk down by asking:
  – What is a part of this?
  – How?
  – What?
  – When?
  – What is an example of this?

Hierarchy of Ideas in the context of Robben Island

Robben Island

- Each higher level contains the detail below it – the question, 'What is this a part of?' can lead to it.

- Each lower level is a part of the classification above it – the question, 'What is a part of this?' can lead to it.

Inspirations

- Watch the Clint Eastwood movie *Invictus*, and/or the documentary *The 16th Man* with Nelson Mandela.

- And/or read the book on which the *Invictus* movie is based, namely *Playing the Enemy – Nelson Mandela and the Game That Made a Nation* by John Carlin (more recent editions of the book are also titled *Invictus*).

- As you enjoy watching the movie or reading the book, note specifically how your understanding and learning about the MadibaMindset deepens.

- Remember that the *Oxford Dictionary* defines 'sell' as 'to inspire someone to possess' and that it suggests inspiration is 'a suggestion coming from an influential person.' With that in mind, do you understand why I stress the importance of the following two points?
  – FW de Klerk made a great sale when he inspired his voters to let go of their fears and seek a new democracy.
  – At least one of Mandela's greatest sales is recorded in *Invictus*.

We can all become better salespeople and many will benefit!

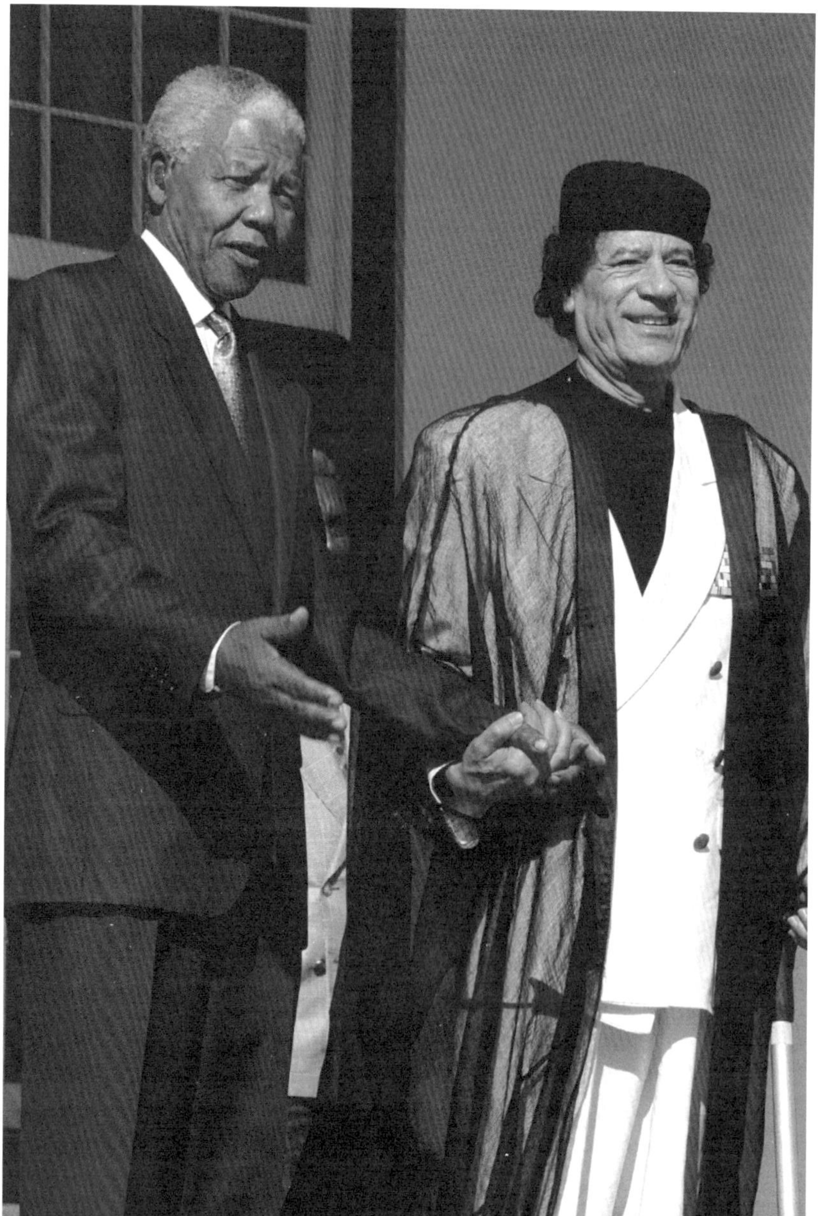

7

Is it final or can we aim for Chapter 11?

A comrade was most upset when a car rental agency issued me with a VW Polo instead of something more suitable for a leader. It's all a matter of values in the end.
AHMED KATHRADA
Memoirs (p. 297)

BEFORE I STARTED WRITING the final chapter of this book my wife noticed that it is numbered seven. I am not sure why this number fell where it did, but coincidentally it represents serious concerns. In the United States final Corporate Bankruptcy is known as 'Chapter 7'. What is the relevance of this coincidence to the present and to the reader? In bankruptcy, the corporation is closed down, operations cease, jobs are lost, and physical assets are sold off as quickly as possible, usually for less than their intrinsic value. When applied to countries this disaster is known as a failed state – a state some countries have already reached. According to the qualification criteria outlined on the Fund for Peace's Failed States Index, Zimbabwe and Somalia top the list in Africa. **At the time of writing most first-world countries are deeply in debt. Politically and internationally this inflection point is being ignored to varying degrees.**

Remember that when your habits, such as materialism or military addictions, are dictating your values, you may also have a failed state – of mind! Apartheid South Africa would probably by now have earned failed state status if the South African Nobel laureates and many others had not recognised the inflection point and acted. The new strategies introduced were based on the values of the Freedom Charter and a Chapter 11 process was initiated. Chapter 11, in the USA, equates with the Business Rescue Process in the new South African Companies Act. At least 20 years ago Mandela, De Klerk and others initiated a State Rescue Process and things started to get better. The goal of this process – whether for a country, a company or a person – is to rebuild, use physical and cerebral assets productively, retain and grow jobs that add value, and reinvest so that the whole process results in a better future. Despite initial progress there is still terrible poverty in South Africa, combined with a lack of skills and an unemployment rate of some 30 per cent amongst the poor. Early in 2010 South Africa was listed at 122 (a higher ranking is better than a low one), after dropping three places since 2008, on the Failed States Index. This ranking is in the section headed **'Warning!'**

Over many years, perhaps since the days of Reaganomics, the people of the USA have lost much of their cherished freedom in an insidious way, going backwards whilst feeling better. This regression has included:

- Living beyond their means and getting into deep debt personally.
- Becoming dependent on a massive amount of imported oil. This dependency is often perpetuated by a belief that the American addict is, for some unknown reason, entitled to use twice as much oil as other nationals. This has contributed to a huge trade deficit and is exacerbated by dependency on a part of the world that is not particularly fond of the USA.
- Consuming more cheap Chinese imports than they need and so becoming massively indebted to a country that has little respect for fair trade, freedom of speech or human rights.

Those concerned talk about all kinds of controls and restrictions to help with the above problems. The real power is with the consumers who can – 'What can I do regardless?' – decide to buy and use less of these products. We have choice in the free world.

I make the above generalisations because, although America is the greatest democracy of the world, this example points to the bad habits of the people: the voters encouraged by self-serving, unsustainable promises of politicians, who have locked their country into these shackles and debt. How will they recognise that this is a state inflection point, and what corrective action will be taken? Will the people mandate Washington that oil consumption should be reduced radically, or just do it? Should gasoline taxes increase by a like amount to balance the budget? This would follow a changed state ... of mind – a big mindshift!

This is not only about the RSA and the USA. We can all face the fact that it is both rich and poor countries that are facing unemployment, inequality, instability and unsustainability. The recent financial crisis helps to highlight that these challenges are almost everywhere to varying degrees. As you read and consider the rest of this chapter, remember that when one country is mentioned the principles and opportunities probably apply to all. Remember the 'Why not both?' quote attributed to Mandela? Recently David Cameron, the new British prime minster, introduced this calculus to budgetary debate, which previously dealt with either cuts or growth. He proposed going for both of the foregoing by cutting wasteful spending, and investing in productivity, so enabling a multiplier effect. It seems so simple before it becomes political!

The leading article in the *Financial Mail* of 19 February 2010 was titled 'State of Collapse' and describes the dysfunctional operations of the following South African public enterprises:

- The South African Broadcasting Corporation: state-owned and collapsing financially although every TV owner must pay a licence fee to it regardless.
- Eskom: a monopoly; mismanaged state-owned electricity generator.
- Transnet: state-owned underperforming operator of railways, pipelines and harbours.
- South African Airways: bankrupt state-owned national airline.
- SA Post Office: state-owned postal monopoly with serious service flaws.

These state enterprises are all providers of critical services upon which the economy and all citizens depend. Their mismanagement appears to stem from political interference in the appointment of CEOs and senior management. That is not putting the consumer or voter first! Author and political commentator Allister Sparks recently wrote that 'everyone in the ANC is ambitious, whether it's for the presidency or just to make a lot of money. The point is that during the liberation struggle there used to be real personal risk and sacrifice in joining the ANC. But now you don't sacrifice anything. You have to join it to get anywhere. It's become a bandwagon of opportunism.' More and more evidence arises of a ruling class addicted to power and materialism.

Despite the service and financial deficiencies of these state-owned operations, the ANC Youth League's leadership persists in calling for the nationalisation of the mines. Presently South African mines are efficiently run businesses, foreign-exchange earners, massive taxpayers and large employers. Is this a ploy to gain power by offering false hope to the unemployed? If so, it can – like the problems outlined in the previous paragraph – also be analysed in terms of the addiction model that applied to apartheid's oppression! Fortunately, because all have a vote, **the voter can change this.** Presently the majority of voters remain loyal based upon reminders that their liberators were members of the once-admirable ANC, upon unkept promises and grants paid to the poorest. South Africa is constitutionally a democracy and when the voters change their state of mind in this regard things can improve.

In a December 2009 *Newsweek* interview Bill Clinton said if 'you ask how do you live with inequality, instability, and unsustainability, my answer is you've got to build the capacity of the poor people of the world and build the flexibility of the rich countries and move away from rigidity.' He was answering a question in the context of future preference – the idea that each person has an obligation to sacrifice today for the benefit of tomorrow, a long-time basic savings principle. No doubt Nelson Mandela is an extreme example of a life totally biased towards future preference. First impressions of recent politics and history suggest that the present bias is sufficiently far in favour of instant gratification so that the future outcome can only be Chapter 7. I suggest that this is not an either/or choice and that the MadibaMindset can be used to balance the present with one's preferred future. David Cameron is the first state leader who I have noticed to clearly articulate this strategy recently. In this context, I ask that you consider the following questions:

What if South Africa and other nations do not embrace and apply the MadibaMindset?

Some unfortunate evidence of the core principles ignored after Mandela stood down as president is already referred to above. The most recent dangerous development is the Protection of Information Bill, which the ANC government is trying to pass into law. It is similar to an old apartheid law called the Official Secrets Act and Kader Asmal – one of the ANC old school who has retained his admirable integrity – recently wrote when describing its abhorrence that this is what 'the Bill should be called'. This law is designed to curb the freedom of the press. The editor of *Finance Week* – in the same edition of 12 August 2010 in which Asmal made his indictment – opined that 'State control of all media will allow the government to abuse its powers without the man in the street knowing about it. But over the long term government will become increasingly ineffective until, as in the former Soviet Union, it finally collapses and drags the whole country down with it.' There is hope that this Bill will be modified somewhat. Nonetheless it reveals a dangerous desire to control and censor. This suggests that leaders do not want ordinary people to make decisions based on a free flow of information.

The heading above is, without being too specific or political, most revealing when asked about all countries, especially those facing employment and financial deficits. The clamour to reduce taxes and simultaneously protect favourite entitlements and military power does not reconcile with values such as personal responsibility, future preference and compassion. Nevertheless, the underlying arithmetic impossibility of this contradiction appears to be extremely popular – at least on both sides of the North Atlantic. Hopefully the inflection point that can be expected will be neither too painful nor far spread.

South Africa can be seen as a microcosm of this situation. It has enjoyed excellent financial leadership since democracy. These leaders' work has however been inhibited by a monopolistic political power alliance in the ANC. The incompatible allies involved were pushed together in the past because they were all oppressed by the old minority government. Now they seem unable to follow their own paths due to fear of loss of power. Are they 'convicted' to their values or not?

The Freedom Charter was designed to transform the nation for the benefit of all citizens, so empowering all South Africans. This can be achieved through good education, skills and job creation, and the delivery of reliable, cost-effective services. In this way all South Africans could prosper from transformation and not just a few, who benefit short-term from union privilege, nationalisation, corruption, or expropriation of public and private funds.

What if they applied the MadibaMindset?
There is good news! One encouraging recent example of the 'What can I do about it regardless?' approach reminds us that **ordinary citizens can produce extraordinary outcomes**. When the December 2009 high-school graduation results were announced in South Africa there was a general outcry (even the president had something to say) and disappointment about the results in general. The media were full of debate and discussion – written, oral and visual – about what is wrong with the education system, the schools, the teachers, and the historic influence of apartheid on education. I was excited to see one article about a poor school achieving a 30-per-cent improvement over 2008 in their pass rate. The teachers were over the moon about these results, having made the extra effort to coach and encourage the learners. Many learners live in shacks without study facilities so the local police station provided a place for them to study. This is an example of how the spirit of each-one-teach-one, even without its reciprocity, can be easily and economically embraced to improve both the context and standards in the essential field of education. I also think that these learners and teachers, having experienced the joy of this self-generated success, will be less likely to vote for dishonest political candidates who offer them something for nothing. This could be because they truly enjoyed earning their educational rewards and using their initiative.

This achievement in education is a wonderful precedent and is predicated on each-one-teach-one and 'What can I do about it regardless?' There are numerous counter examples to the downside under the first heading above, which harmonise with the principles of the MadibaMindset. Let's consider, and be inspired to replicate and encourage, after we read the glowing report on the success of the 2010 Soccer World Cup by John Carlin and published by iol.co.za on 9 July 2010. It includes: 'Someone who works high up in the Local Organising Committee told me how at first it had been a big culture shock to work with these Swiss, they did not understand each other at all. But in time they established a rapport and the fusing of African ebullience with old European discipline ended up doing the job admirably!' Unfortunately FIFA made off with most of the profit from the event. All that needs to happen now is to bring the same spirit of each-one-teach-one to international business ventures and to combine it with a fair sharing of the mutually added value.

George W Bush and Dick Cheney proved that unilateral attacks produce negative results, make the world more dangerous for all, and are prohibitively expensive. Fortunately the US administration learned this lesson and is avoiding it patiently and with determination in dealing with Iran. Ably assisted by his erstwhile foe, having recognised her essential goodness and ability, Barack Obama worked hard with Hillary Clinton to build an international United Nations sanctions package that included the support of both China and Russia. The result is that many nations have enforced the sanctions more strictly than before and Iran has been caught off guard. The ANC was able to get international support for sanctions against South Africa because their cause was then moral and ethical. This is what is happening to Iran now; hopefully it will result in improved safety for the world and a better life for Iranians.

How much could have been saved, both financially and in terms of human life, if Bush had listened and learned when Mandela spoke out against attacking Iraq? Perhaps the US can today muster more humility, and learn something from England, which delivers medical care at half the cost they do. David Cameron is working to improve on that. Assuming a US state economy approximates the size of Britain's, then each state can, in the spirit of each-one-teach-one, and looking for the good, emulate what works well in the UK system.

What can both the richer European nations and poorer developing nations learn from the unsustainable debt of Greece? The Greek situation seems to have been brought about by its citizens' addiction to entitlement: work fewer hours at higher rates for fewer years, pay no taxes, and receive big pensions, as well as other benefits from the state. This is a great lesson that nothing comes for free and everything has to be paid for. To be sustainable, all who are able are required to contribute more than they take, because there will always be a few who need help – a simple equation in which both the capitalists and the socialists can find common ground.

A report from Athens on 6 August 2010 was headed 'Good start on Greek austerity'. Perhaps the Greeks rioted to get rid of their frustration and disappointment before they started to implement their new and painful austerity programme as agreed. This is further proof that the ebullient and disciplined can develop rapport when challenged, and work together towards a mutually beneficial outcome. Perhaps we can all learn to be both.

We can now be entirely convinced that we can teach ourselves productive habits by emulating others. Start with some South African Nobel laureates. For example, retired South African Archbishop Desmond Tutu's habits were recently described in *Perfect Weekend*, a book authored by Dominique Herman. He evidently regularly goes for 30-minute walks at the age of 78 (physical fitness, a core element of the MadibaMindset), and is quoted in the book as saying: 'I usually have people that I am praying for and I use the walk to think of them. But sometimes my mind goes off and it sees a beautiful girl and you're not concentrating' (mental fitness). Presently the preponderance of reporting on South African leaders is about their expensive cars and flashy lifestyles – usually paid for by the taxpayer. This leaves the impression of a fat-cat lifestyle that cannot encourage frugality in the younger generation. It is more important to encourage the financial, mental and physical fitness aspirations that are so clearly illustrated by the examples of Mandela, De Klerk and Tutu.

Presently there is a shortage of skills in South Africa and it is not easy to find good artisans and other skilled workers in the informal and small business sectors. I have however experienced success in training unskilled people to do productive work and achieve high quality and reliability. I believe that the core habits of the MadibaMindset, as outlined previously, are an essential indigenous 'skill set' available to weave into the fabric of society in South Africa and internationally. This can form the basis of the building of the capacity of the poor, as well as the flexibility required of South Africa, the richest nation on the African continent, to move away from rigidity in sectors such as the labour market. Professor George Devenish wrote recently that *Invictus* is a reminder of Madiba's legacy and how today's leaders let us down. Sadly, I agree with this statement. Why not **embrace this legacy**?

Is it final or can we aim for Chapter 11?

The movie *Invictus*, starring Morgan Freeman and Matt Damon, is based on one of the miracles of Mandela's leadership, which helped South Africa win the Rugby World Cup in 1995. This movie has many meanings, both explicit and covert, and I stress the following:

- The South African team was reputed to be inferior – in skills, training and experience – to their New Zealand opponents who were the favourites to win. Mandela inspired his team and their captain. They rose to the occasion, performed above themselves, and won.
- Rugby was the sport of the Afrikaner oppressor. The majority of the South African population supported neither rugby nor the national team. Most of the Afrikaner minority, who had previously controlled the country, were suspicious of their new president and doubted that he was for them. Mandela used his personal support of the South African team in the World Cup to inspire all South African citizens. His highly visible desire to work for all was immediately apparent and his people united behind him. At the final World Cup match the spectators all rose to the occasion and together they chanted 'Nelson! Nelson! Nelson!' and there was a miraculous reconciliation.

Both *Invictus* and the 2010 Soccer World Cup show that with competent leadership, based on the principles of the MadibaMindset, a challenged country can perform better than its history and form predict. This is true of individuals as well. Presently South Africa, and its human capital, are underperforming in many areas, including education and training, health and productivity, safety and security, economic and export growth. As I wrote previously, all these deficits, and more, can be reduced when citizens and leaders **embrace the legacy of the MadibaMindset**. The answer to the question 'What if they had done it?' is that South Africa would today be healthier, wiser, wealthier and happier. Remember that Mandela did not succumb to the government for as long as he was opposed to it. Every day in prison he is reputed to have recited the poem *Invictus* by British poet William Ernest Henley. The last verse of the poem declares:

It matters not how strait the gate,
How charged with punishments the scroll.
I am the master of my fate:
I am the captain of my soul.

One of the human race's most irrational and unresourceful habits is to want a new outcome and simultaneously continue to do the same failing strategy – or more of the same things as before. How can we expect the same behaviour – such as voting for leaders who are already letting us down – to suddenly produce a new result? Chapter 3 recorded how we can recognise inflection points. Chapter 4 suggested that we write down what we want to achieve, and how we can plan to achieve it in terms of our personal freedom charter. If you did not write **your freedom charter** and apply it, and/or if you don't do it, then it is highly unlikely that you will achieve something new or different. Sometimes, even when you do what you planned, you don't get the desired result. That is why in Chapter 4 we suggested that you can be flexible and change your inputs!

What if YOU embrace and apply the MadibaMindset?

My experience and what I truly believe can happen for you, the reader, when you start doing the MadibaMindset and develop congruent habits, is: You can become progressively healthier, wiser, wealthier and happier! It is a sequential process, probably with many ups and downs, and challenges as well as happiness, as the new direction becomes clear and the new habits entrench themselves. As you continue doing it I wish you success, however you define it, in accordance with your sustainable and worthwhile values, on your own journey!

In this way countries, corporations and individuals can avoid Chapter 7. Perhaps you need to start at Chapter 11 (the Business Rescue stage) and change your state ... of mind. By your own design and by this act, you can turn yourself towards more success. Once you start achieving that success – material or otherwise (which is by no means immaterial) – remember that, as Bill Clinton and many others have said and experienced, the danger can be rigidity.

In the same spirit, I sincerely wish that, mandated and guided by their voters, the governments of this world can meet unique and

Is it final or can we aim for Chapter 11?

unprecedented challenges, both present and future, with creativity and flexibility – perhaps embracing the MadibaMindset where appropriate. The optimist within me relishes the thought of reading this again and again over the years and celebrating that its warnings have become redundant as their darkness is obliterated by new and repetitive enlightenment!

Apply the MadibaMindset flexibly and be sure to look after the interests of the less fortunate, at which stage real wealth and happiness are earned.

Appendix A

Aiming higher

JAMES MCINTOSH

THE REASONS GIVEN IN Chapter 1 for becoming a user of the MadibaMindset might seem compelling; however, none of these reasons explain **how** it was possible for Mandela and his colleagues to survive the oppressive conditions in prison and to be released triumphant with their convictions undimmed. To understand how that was even remotely possible, we need to explore a few basic ideas of behavioural psychology.

There are different schools of psychological thinking that attempt to explain human behaviour. Some, like the psychoanalytic theories of Sigmund Freud, Carl Jung and Erik Erikson, propose that inner factors (subconscious or biological) drive one's behaviour. Others, like BF Skinner's Classical Conditioning (Pavlov's Dog and Bell experiment) and Albert Bandura's Social Learning Theory, argue that all behaviour is learned behaviour.

The central tenet of the humanists' theories is that man can be 'more than he is'. They see man as a responsible being, able to choose freely from the possibilities available to him, always striving to realise his potential and to be truly himself. In this sense, man is a being who is not complete, but is a work in progress, in the process of becoming. The common thread of these theories is the emphasis on the drive for growth and the search for meaning as motivations of human behaviour. Viktor Frankl called this 'man's search for meaning';

Abraham Maslow called it 'self-actualisation'; and Carl Rogers called it 'wholeness, the development of all potential, to become that self which one truly is'.

The humanist theories do not ignore biological needs or the influence of the environment. Rather, the humanists see developmental drives as being of greater significance. The instinct for survival (biological needs) will drive behaviour until it has been satisfied, at which stage the developmental needs will demand attention.

Of interest to the users of the MadibaMindset is the idea that some people are able to ignore or suppress their biological needs in favour of their developmental needs. Remember the words that Nelson Mandela spoke at his treason trial? 'But if needs be, it is an ideal for which I am prepared to die.' In other words, this 'need' of his, the need to see all men equal, was greater than his basic needs for food, shelter and safety. In fact, it was a greater need than his need to live (without this equality). Let us now explore how it is possible for this level of conviction to exist at all.

Become all you can be

Abraham Maslow distinguished between five needs: physiological needs; security needs; the need for love, acceptance and belonging; the need for esteem and appreciation; and the need for self-actualisation. He arranged these needs in a hierarchy to reflect each need's relative potency. According to this theory, a higher need is experienced only once the preceding lower need has been satisfied, or at least partially satisfied to the extent that the person feels assured that this need will be satisfied in the future.

Physiological needs, such as the need for food and water, are the most basic needs. These are also the strongest needs in that if they remain unsatisfied, no other need is likely to be experienced. Try to imagine what it must be like in a prison such as Robben Island, where some days it must feel as if not even your most basic needs for survival are being met. Can you imagine somehow remaining focused on your dream of freedom, not for yourself alone, but for all people?

Security needs include the need for order, protection, stability and freedom from fear and anxiety. The need for love, acceptance and belonging is reflected in the need to receive and give love within loving relationships, and in the need to be a member of a group or to identify with a group of people. The need for self-esteem is the need to evaluate oneself positively, which mainly comes from feeling respected and appreciated by others.

The final need in the hierarchy is the need for self-actualisation. This has to do with personal growth and development in that it is the desire to become all one is capable of becoming. This need is intrinsically motivated and unique to each one of us, for we must each discover what this need means for us individually and then satisfy the need for ourselves.

As with any theory, there are always a few individuals who, probably not having heard of Maslow and his ideas, do not behave accordingly. Noted examples are Nelson Mandela, Mother Teresa and Mahatma Gandhi. People like these live for what they believe in, often at the expense of their lower needs, such as their physiological and safety needs. In terms of Maslow's theory, they are said to 'self-actualise'.

We may think that these people are unique, unlikely to be found in large numbers doing routine work. That is correct, but only up to a point. We tend to forget that individuals such as search-and-rescue personnel, aid workers, war correspondents, and even those who participate in less risky activities such as blowing the whistle on corporate wrong-doing, protesting against war, globalisation and environmental deterioration, all seem to place their personal beliefs above their personal safety needs. And what do you say of suicide bombers? You might not agree with either their beliefs or their actions, and yet their actions speak of a belief powerful enough to overcome all lower-level needs.

This does seem to point to a level even beyond merely becoming all that you can be, to a level that has to do with a search for personal meaning, a level that embraces a willingness to die for beliefs.

Searching for meaning
Viktor Frankl was already a well-known psychiatrist and neurologist when he was imprisoned during 1944 and 1945 in several Nazi concentration camps, including Auschwitz and Dachau. It is there that he observed that the questions his fellow prisoners asked most frequently related to the meaning of life. He noted that the need to find meaning and the need to go on believing in something seemed to

be more urgent than other needs, such as the need for food or safety, even though these were in painfully short supply. In his book *Man's Search for Meaning: An Introduction to Logotherapy*, Frankl wrote that he and other prisoners became 'disgusted' that their situation compelled them to think 'only of such trivial things'.

No doubt, it was these personal experiences that led Frankl to believe that, above all, we humans want meaning in life. Irrespective of the circumstances, Frankl believed that the desire to find meaning (the will-to-meaning) will always be the strongest motivator of human behaviour. Consider how often we hear about a rich and successful person who is depressed, even though his or her basic needs for ease and safety have been satisfied. Frankl felt strongly that the behaviour of people like Nelson Mandela, Mother Teresa and Mahatma Gandhi is far more common. In fact, he felt so strongly about this that he rejected Maslow's views of a hierarchy of needs. Instead, Frankl argued in another book (*The Unheard Cry for Meaning: Psychotherapy and Humanism*) that if lower needs are **not** satisfied, then a higher need, such as the will-to-meaning, may actually become more important.

Actually, Frankl went much further than merely rejecting Maslow's theories. He firmly believed that the central issue faced by man is not the struggle to survive, but the struggle to find meaning in life. Man wants to feel that he has achieved something with his life; above all, he does not want to feel that his life is meaningless. Frankl suggested that there are three levels or dimensions, which together make up man's existence, namely physical, psychological and spiritual. The physical level explains our basic functioning as any living biological organism. The psychological level explains our behaviour in terms of needs, drives and other abilities, which barely distinguishes us from other animals. However, the spiritual level sets man apart and is viewed by Frankl (and by existentialists) as the most important:

| *Man wills for (seeks) meaning:* | Man inherently wants to live a meaningful life. He wants his life to reflect ideals and values more meaningful than merely the satisfying of needs and drives, even to the extent that he would be prepared to die for his ideals and the people he loves. |

Man has freedom of will:	Biological and psychological laws govern man's behaviour on the physical and psychological levels. But on the spiritual plane, man has freedom of will. This freedom of will allows man to actively resist the influences operating at the lower levels. This means that man constantly faces choices, specifically about his attitude in any given circumstance – what Frankl calls the last of the human freedoms.
Man has responsibility:	This freedom of will comes at a 'price': man may be held responsible for his choices. He cannot excuse his behaviour by blaming it on lower level influences or even on external circumstances. All he can say is that he chose to give in to his drives.

No doubt, many people, including behaviourists and psychologists, more readily accept the last two characteristics and are less comfortable with the first one. Some behaviourists and psychologists even suggest that the will-to-meaning should be regarded as no more than the rationalisation of hidden drives or suppressed instincts. But consider what Frankl asked and then decide for yourself:

Are you willing to live merely according to your hidden drives?
Are you willing to die for your suppressed instincts?
Or might you be willing to live according to, and even to die for, what you believe in?

Staying convicted – a matter of self-respect

Even Maslow acknowledged that some people manage to 'ignore' their other needs as they attempt to self-actualise, to become all they can be. However, not many of us are able to aim straight at the level of self-actualisation, the way people like Mandela, Gandhi and Mother Theresa did. Most of us need to work through our hierarchy of needs. The point, though, is that there is no reason for us to stay trapped at any lower level. No one traps us; we trap ourselves.

Aiming higher

What has this to do with self-respect? Well, one of the traps we fall into is the trap of self-esteem based on our self-serving bias. When we view success or good outcomes as a result of our own doing or personal characteristics – that is self-serving bias. When we blame failure or bad outcomes on external causes or bad luck – self-serving bias again. Why do we do this? According to psychologists, if we can claim responsibility for good things, then our self-esteem and our public image are enhanced. And if we can blame failure on external factors then we can protect our self-esteem and our public image.

That is why, when things don't work out the way we want them to, we look to blame politicians, the economy, greedy bankers, ex-bosses, ex-spouses, and so on. The problem with blame is that it really only makes you feel better for a short period of time. And then you must get back to doing something about your situation. Blame might keep your self-esteem intact. However, your self-respect demands that you take responsibility for doing something about your situation.

You will only be free to be yourself, to live with conviction, to become all that you can be, when what you stand for matters more to you than what others think; when your need for self-respect is stronger than the need for the respect of others; and when your desire for self-actualisation is stronger than the need for self-esteem.

According to Maslow's hierarchy of needs, if a lower-level need unexpectedly became unsatisfied, you could find yourself again operating at that lower need level. Undoubtedly, users of the MadibaMindset will find it much easier to prevent a slide to lower levels. They will keep their self-respect intact as they stay focused on what has meaning. In other words, users of the Madiba Mindset will find it easier to live with conviction.

Appendix B

Important readers' questions and author's replies

Liz: The well-known personalities and pithy quotes you incorporate vibrantly bring the text alive as you guide us to use these same principles in realising our own dreams. It is both more interesting and entertaining than a straight self-help book. To fully appreciate the contents, a fairly high level of thinking and functioning is required. I am not sure if this is your intention and if so whether it unnecessarily limits its audience.

Tyrrel: This book is only a start. My dream is to find a way to fund special rewrites to align with age and education levels of readers. Translations into mother tongues can also be extremely useful. Training courses are also being considered.

Liz: The final chapter, however, tends to place the book firmly in the political arena – whether all readers will benefit from this is debatable. Having said that, the examples and opinions offered are interesting and in the final paragraphs the points raised are tied into the MadibaMindset philosophy.

Tyrrel: If the book can stimulate vigorous and productive debate I am very pleased. Debate can bring constructive opinions and actions to the fore. It is not about my opinions but rather a method as described in the last sentence of Mike Nicol's preface. This book describes an empowering method to exemplify that it is what we make out of what we have, not what we are given, that separates one person from another.

Acknowledgements

I learned about modelling and NLP in America, and thank all my teachers of this discipline. This was around the time of the 1994 democratic election and I read *Long Walk to Freedom*. I became curious about what could be modelled from this event and the history and heroes behind it. I started to write a training course.

Then I met Derrick Grootboom at a tourism show in Durban. He was conducting tours of Robben Island; we got on well, and I saw the opportunity to combine this with my idea of a teaching course. He arrived on the island before he had finished high school and achieved his matriculation – high-school graduation – during his time of incarceration. After his release he studied Law at the University of the Western Cape and graduated. Later he was awarded a Nelson Mandela Scholarship to study in the United Kingdom where he earned a master's degree. He was appointed assessor in the High Court of Cape Town and is simultaneously developing his own entrepreneurial initiatives. He is rising above financial challenges and has been stimulated both by his Robben Island graduation, his education and his experience in England. He is committed to teach others as he continues his struggle for the economic liberation of all South Africans.

Dorria Watt of KC Public Relations came up with the name MadibaMindset.

Indres Naidoo later helped with some presentations when Derrick withdrew. Bryan Rostron writes of Indres: 'Sometimes when I feel disenchanted – I think of Indres and that unquenchable generosity of spirit. In particular, I remember an evening at his flat high above Cape Town, a few days after New Year, with two other celebrated ex-Island graduates [Mac Maharaj, a Minister in our first democratic government and Mandela's close confidant Ahmed Kathrada] plus

Denis Goldberg, tried with Mandela at the celebrated Rivonia Trial, but who as a white had been incarcerated in Pretoria. These were some of South Africa's longest serving political prisoners, yet in the early hours they started swapping jail yarns and laughing their heads off. I went onto Indres' balcony with its breathtaking view over the lit-up city. Out in the dark of the bay, just visible, were lights from Robben Island, and I remember thinking. "Yes, to have lived to experience this ..."'

Bryan Rostron reminded me over the years that it was a good idea, although writing books was seldom financially profitable.

James McIntosh brought structure and a 'third mind' to the whole effort, as well as helping with research, doing electronic publishing, and more.

Geraldene Corder edited, questioned, marked-up, re-edited, formatted, reformatted, and questioned more!

Sarah Corder drew the profile reproduced on these pages.

Mike Nicol did a reader's report, wrote the preface, gave advice, and encouraged me to finish.

My wife Jean accepts when I am 'not there' and engrossed, and encourages and supports the effort.

I thank all of these people and the each-one-teach-one experience we enjoyed. We have all learned from each other and all were invaluable in completing this DIY production. Also all the others, friends and foes, with whom I have experienced ubuntu in action.

Tyrrel Fairhead
August 2011

Suggested reading

Books

Carlin, John. *Playing the Enemy*, Atlantic, 2009.

Chandler, Alfred. 'Strategy and structure.' In *Resources, Firms and Strategies*, edited by Nicolai J. Foss, Oxford University Press, 2003.

Crwys-Williams, Jennifer (ed). *In the Words of Nelson Mandela*, Penguin, 2010.

Frankl, Viktor. *Man's Search for Meaning: An Introduction to Logotherapy*, Rider & Co, 2008.

Frankl, Viktor. *The Unheard Cry for Meaning: Psychotherapy and Humanism*, Touchstone, 1975.

Gladwell, Malcolm. *Outliers*, Penguin, 2008.

Grove, Andrew. *Only The Paranoid Survive*, Broadway Business, 1999.

Hamilton, Alexander. *Writings*, Library of America, 2001.

Herman, Dominique. *Perfect Weekend*, Art, 2010.

Hill, Napoleon. *Think and Grow Rich*, Random House, 1987.

Huxley, Aldous. *Brave New World Revisited*, HarperCollins, 2000.

Janjigian, Vahan. *Even Buffet is Not Perfect*, Penguin, 2009.

Kathrada, Ahmed. *Memoirs*, Zebra, 2004.

Laborde, Genie. *Influencing with Integrity*, Crown House, 1995.

Mandela, Nelson. *Long Walk to Freedom*, Little, Brown and Company, 1994.

Naidoo, Indres. *Island in Chains*, Penguin, 2000.

Nicol, Mike, et al. *Mandela – The Authorised Portrait*, Wild Dog, 2009.

Poiter, Sidney. *The Measure of a Man*, Simon & Schuster UK Ltd, 2000.

Robbins, Anthony. *Unlimited Power*, Ballantine, 1987.

Sampson, Anthony. *Mandela – The Authorised Biography*, HarperCollins, 1999.
Stengel, Richard. *Mandela's Way*, Virgin, 2010.
Wareham, John. *How to Break Out of Prison*, Welcome Rain, 2002.
Wilson, Francis. *Dinosaurs, Diamonds and Democracy*, Umuzi, 2009.

Websites

Finance Week: www.fin24.com
Financial Mail: www.financialmail.co.za
Freedom Charter: www.sahistory.org.za/pages/governence-projects/freedom-charter
Fund for Peace's Failed State Index: www.fundforpeace.org and www.foreignpolicy.com
Independent Online: www.iol.co.za
MadibaMindset: www.madibamindset.com
Nelson Mandela Foundation: www.nelsonmandela.org
Sunday Times: www.timeslive.co.za
Time magazine: www.time.com